The Little Blue Book on Writing Well and Getting Published

Proven Methods, Tips, And Tools

Dr. Chris E. Stout

ISBN-13: 978-1502928276

WHAT OTHERS ARE SAYING ABOUT CHRIS

He is "...one of the most frequently cited psychologists in the scientific literature." *Hartwick College*

<>

"(we) appreciate Dr. Chris Stout's outstanding service to the nation as a member of the Baldrige national quality program evaluation team for healthcare." *(the late) Ronald H. Brown, United States Secretary of Commerce*

<>

"We are indeed grateful to you...(for) having been in the forefront of advocacy throughout the years, and to have helped to create and shape psychology." *Richard M. Suinn, PhD, APA President 1998-9, and Jack Wiggins, PhD, APA President 1992-3*

<>

"Chris is a true model for not only his young peers to emulate, but for all of us to admire." *Stephen Pfeiffer, PhD, Executive Director, AAP*

<>

"(Chris)is results-oriented, has a positive mind, is generous and true. This guy is a star." *Dominique-Henri Freiche Paris*

<>

"There is optimism and vulnerability that filter through Chris' world view and suffuse his work. His energy is respectful of others and hopeful for the world and we are all better for it." *Leigh W. Jerome, PhD Hawaii*

"From Forrest Gump (with a brain) to entrepreneur and global missionary. Nice! God bless you and your work." *Drew Edwards, EdD*

"More action, and less rhetoric, to improve the health and well-being of people is a fruitful approach to global peace. Chris should be commended for his systematically working toward his goals." *Dan Leviton, PhD, U. Of Maryland*

"When I first met Chris, it was at the TED conference in Monterey. We had a brief discussion which has impacted my life ever since. One phrase, 'do important things' changed how I look at who I am, what I do in life, and how it effects others. From minor activities to large projects, I now view them in a different context. This adds depth and new textures to my actions which were previously unavailable to how I lived in the real world." *Ted Stout (not related), ROI*

"Impressive and inspiring. Very fast with hard core heart and guts galore. This is a man who is truly paying it forward and providing human-kind the resources for generative change across the globe." *Bill Denne, LCSW*

"Chris Stout is a remarkable man. He has the intellect of Bernard Baruch, the fearlessness of Evel Knievel and the affability of Bill Clinton." *Ralph Musicant, JD, Harvard Law*

"Strong in the face of adversity, thoughtful, kind, conscientious, compassionate, intelligent and inspiring! What a world it would be if only we could say that Chris Stout's story is a norm." *Debbie Carvalko, Praeger Publishers*

"It is inspirational to see someone accomplish as much as Chris has, and then keep right on going." *Leslie Piotrowski, Lake County Health Department*

<>

"Dr. Stout a wonderful example of how creativity, discipline, fierce intelligence, and genuine caring can together move the world in extraordinary new directions." *D. R. Baerger, PhD, JD, Chicago*

<>

"Dr. Stout's experiences have brought to him a level of understanding I can only hope to aspire to one day." *Andrew Garman, PsyD, MA, Rush University*

"Chris' story has brought tears to my eyes - tears of admiration, inspiration, and encouragement. It is not easy for any of us to take the initiative, to move outside of comfortable boundaries, to want to change the world and to do something active, risky and meaningful to make a difference. Chris seems well on his way to making his life a true contribution to the lives of others." *Fields Wicker-Miurin, London*

"I met Chris on a 1997 flying doctors mission to Vietnam. He is one of the most genuine and impressive people I've met. He walks the talk. A gem." *Nancy Beahm Koritz, Tokyo*

"I have known Chris for almost 20 years and I am still consistently amazed by his energy, sincerity, intellect and humility. He is an unparalleled dreamer and doer. There have been many times when I was inspired by his worldview and felt privileged simply to be in his company. There are not many people who can say that they left the world a better place than they found it, but Chris is certainly one of them." *Cam Helkowski, MA, Loyola University*

"Dr. Stout's vision is compassionate, creative and sizzling with energy. A truly inspirational leader!" *Giovanni Caracci, MD, New York City*

Dedication

This book is dedicated to you as a reader *and* writer along with my thanks for your interest it and my hope that it will prove useful in your passion for words. – CES

CONTENTS

Acknowledgments

My thanks to Hanying Wang, MS, for all of her help and amazing skill that went into the creation of the manuscript. There are folks much more talented than I writing on this topic, and thankfully they have agreed to contribute their ideas, tips, and expertise as well! I so appreciate not only their talent, but also their generosity to share as contributing chapter authors. It is a who's-who of content experts and thought leaders in their areas of expertise. Thanks to Bryan Tracy, Kivi Leroux Miller, Brian Feinblum, Lindsay Buroker, Zepho Inc Marketing Team, Ryan Deiss, CreateSpaceResources, Steve O'Keefe, and Guy Kawasaki.

Foreword

Chris' adventuresome life has taken him to a variety of exotic and often not-so-safe locals and it is through the work he has done in these venues that resulted in his Center for Global Initiatives. He has done well with many of the aspects I wrote about in *Never Eat Alone* but applied them in the milieu of humanitarian work. He and I share a kinship as Chris was a reviewer for the Abe awards that I founded, as a fellow Baldrige Award Reviewer, we were both "TEDizens" during the Richard Saul Wurman era, along with both having been elected as a Global Leader of Tomorrow by the World Economic Forum and serving as faculty in Davos.

While Chris is able to contribute to Davos talks and UN presentations, he is much more comfortable working in the field and with his students. He is known for bringing together people in cross-disciplinary projects world-wide—in healthcare, medical education, human rights, poverty, conflict, policy, sustainable development, diplomacy, and terrorism.   *– Keith Ferrazzi , Ferrazzi Greenlight*

Chapter 1

Introduction

By Chris E. Stout

Off to a Great Start!

I am so happy that you have this book! Congratulations as you now have a great Tool Box that has been key to what I have learned in my writing and publishing career.

If you like what you're reading, then please check out my other books at http://tinyurl.com/StoutOnAmazon

And here are some additional links and resources:

➢ Follow my Linkedin Influencer blogs and add your own comments at:

http://www.linkedin.com/influencer/3055695

➢ If you are looking to make a REAL difference in the world, then welcome!

Http://CenterForGlobalInitiatives.org

➢ Professionally connect @

http://www.linkedin.com/in/drchrisstout/

➢ Friend @ https://www.facebook.com/#!/drchrisstout

➢ Follow @ http://pinterest.com/drchrisstout/

➢ Follow @ https://twitter.com/drchrisstout

And of course, please always feel free to contact me personally at: Http://DrChrisStout.com

I love to read. I love to write. But it's hard to do either

with my learning disability. And as you may know, it can be hard to write even without a learning disability.

Over the years I developed tools (or hacks) to compensate, and now you have them. I hope you may find them useful in your work. I always imagined myself as the love-child of Ayn Rand and William F. Buckley, Jr., vis-à-vis their amazing vocabulary and incredible skill as stringing big words together (not so much their politics). I have also learned a lot about publishing over the past 25 years and I thought that sharing and demystifying all that could also be of interest to others.

While I still cannot spell worth a hoot, I have a rockin' vocabulary and that was thanks to these tools. Basically, when I read or hear a word or a phrase that I liked (or was puzzled by), I wrote it down. If it was new to me I then looked it up and wrote that down as well. All of these phrases, big words, and a boat-load of helpful quotes appear in the appendices, enjoy!

The result of all this…?

- Publication of over 35 books (by *REAL* publishing houses like Wiley, Praeger, APA, ABC-CILO, Greenwood Press, Springer-Verlag, Charles C. Thomas…),

- Intimate knowledge and a great deal of experience with those top publishers, their contracts, expectations, etc…,

- Over 100 peer reviewed professional, scientific journal manuscripts published,

- Over 200 professional presentations…

- … in most every state and more than 15 countries,

- Being translated into Russian, Turkish, Korean, Mandarin, Spanish, Polish, Arabic, and French, and

- Blogging as a Linkedin Influencer with over 10,000 followers.

Now it's YOUR turn…! And holler if I can be of help.

SECTION I

Basics

Chris E. Stout

Chapter 2

Getting Started

By Chris E. Stout

Nonfiction Books

My writing to this point has been exclusively nonfiction, thus my perspective is informed from the experiences in this realm. Having said that, however, many aspects of this book are nevertheless applicable—such as contracts, marketing, even the vocabulary tips—however, I believe it is a more common practice to seek the assistance of an agent for pitching a fiction manuscript or screenplay, as those are generally finished works. In working with traditional publishing houses like Wiley, Praeger, Greenwood, etc., I have found it extraordinarily more helpful to first have an articulated and fleshed-out idea, a sample table of contents, and a sample chapter to pitch to a traditional publisher. (I have given examples of these in Chapter 9.)

Reviewing

But what if a book seems too daunting to start with, or you simply aren't ready with enough to say for a book-sized manuscript? Serving as a peer reviewer is a great way to get started as a professional. As such you need not feel the pressure of publication as most peer reviews of journal manuscripts are not meant to be published themselves. You gain an opportunity to see the good and the bad and make recommendations as to how to improve the reviewed piece.

Some publications, such as psychology's *PsychCritiques*, require the reviewer to write a publishable review that is annotated with its own supporting references. I started out writing reviews for *Science Books and Films* and very much enjoyed doing so as well as gaining the experience. If you are in an academic setting such work is additionally helpful in building your curriculum vitae.

Scientific Journals

Speaking of academic settings, publishing in highly ranked, peer reviewed journals are the (academic) gold standard and one's longevity in an academic department is predicated on such productivity as it is generally related to enhancing the prestige of the institution and grant dollars. This then begat the term "Publish or Perish" to indicate that if you did not publish, your tenure in the department would not be very long, and perhaps likewise your academic career.

My undergraduate mentor once told a story of how much he'd worked on a study and was able to finally get it published. When he showed his proud father the paper and related the toil that it took to produce and the competition to overcome to get it published, his father displayed it on the family mantle, and then asked him how much he was paid for such an immense amount of work. The answer, as you may already know, is zero! It's hard to explain this seemingly illogical situation to those outside of academia, but the currency for promotion and security is publishing. Plus, for the author, there is a keen satisfaction of adding to the body of knowledge.

Professional Presentations

It is not uncommon for nascent ideas or preliminary findings to be presented before they are published. This is a wonderful way to gain other's input and criticism that may indeed improve your work and add to your ideas from gaining fresh perspectives of others. Additionally, if is not uncommon for a symposium of topical presentations to be developed into a book. This was the case a few years ago when I was asked to be part of a day long seminar as part of an annual meeting. It was such a great experience the conveners decided to invite interested presenters to write-up their presentations and they were able to secure a contract from a publisher for an edited work. It was a wonderful collaborative addition to presenting.

Professional Magazines

Professional magazines may also be a venue to seek publishing your work. While they do not hold to the same rigger of peer review as scientific journals, they do undergo editorial review and by no means is acceptance for publication something that is "automatically" given for submitting. The value here is that you hone your ideas and writing to a different group of readers and you are able to reach perhaps even a broader audience. For me, this has taken the form of publishing in *Modern Healthcare, The Illinois Psychologist,* and Division 42 of the American Psychological Association's *The Independent Practitioner.*

Freelancing

While all of these aforementioned areas are unpaid, there may be some opportunities to write in your area of expertise as a freelance writer. I did this for a number of years for various monthly newsletters as a columnist and I found it very fulfilling. The payment was minimal and not really the motivation, but again, the venue to have a voice was terrific. (Dinosaur warning: I must admit, this was pre-blogging, and thus there were not, back then, the great opportunities to reach an audience as there is today.) I also wrote content for a behavioral health website on contract, and learned how difficult it can be to write jargon-free at an eighth-grade reading level.

Interesting Combination

I have a colleague who told the story of how he had won a significant grant to study an important area of American life. He did a wonderful study and published his subsequent findings in a respected journal and gave a note of appreciation to the funding source for the grant dollars. He then took his findings and authored a book that was written to a lay-audience that could likewise benefit from his findings, and gained book royalties from that publication.

Writing versus Editing

You may have an idea for a book topic but not enough material for more than a chapter or two. However, you may have colleagues that would be interested in contributing to such a work. This then is a wonderful way to tackle a book project and not feel too overwhelmed. The issues to be careful with are internal and external.

Internally, you will need more time than it may seem, so always add a buffer and be willing to be super-strict as to self-discipline of your time and other demands upon you. You need to be a very detail oriented person and also realize that while you may not have written a chapter that you are reviewing, YOU may be the person to edit it into shape. Personally, I have had some situations where I was editing a book and a chapter author's writing was so poor that I could not fix it. I can tell you that is a very uncomfortable conversation to have with someone. A good solution is to recommend a writing coach/consultant, but nevertheless, that may be hard for an author to hear.

Externally, corralling and herding your contributing authors may be as dime consuming as writing the chapters yourself. If at all possible, select authors who have a good track record of publishing, and be super-clear as to timeline expectations. One delinquent contributor can derail your entire book's target date to be submitted, which then fouls up many other aspects like catalog listings, availability at important national meetings where the publisher is exhibiting, etc.

Chapter 3

How to Write a Book

By Bryan Tracy

You have the ability, right now, to write and publish a book on a subject that is important to you. Like riding a bicycle, learning how to write a book is a skill that you can master with practice and repetition.

According to USA Today, 82% of adults dream of writing a book someday, either to express a heart-felt concern about a subject, or to earn a living, and even become successful.

Many books are written by people who are not particularly good at writing. Instead, they hire a "writer-for-hire" who interviews them, takes notes on their ideas and insights, and then works it into a book which they go on to publish under their own name.

Many of the best-selling books on the New York Times lists were not written by the person whose name appears on the cover. They were written by other writers.

There are more than 200,000 books published each year and yours can be one of them.

The key to writing a book is to "Just Write!" Writing is one thing that you cannot get worse at by doing it.

Albert Hubbard, one of the most prolific writers in American history was once asked the key to successful writing. He replied, "The only way to learn to write is to write and write and write and write, and write and write and write."

My own story might be instructive. I did not graduate from high school, and I failed high school English. I fantasized about writing a book for many years before I decided to "Just write!"

In 1981, I began giving talks and seminars to ever larger groups. To speak effectively, I had to do hundreds of hours of research, and read hundreds of books over the years. To keep current, I read dozens of magazines and thousands of articles. I'd read many of them several times.

When I developed my one-to-three day seminars, I would structure the materials so that the seminar started strong, in the first session, and then developed progressively, step-by-step through to the last session, where it ended on a strong, positive note.

When I began to write books, I used the same structure. I learned later that this is a powerful formula for successful books. Start with a strong chapter that gives a lot of value and benefits to the reader, develop the subject throughout the book, and end with a strong chapter that summarizes and emphasizes the main points. It is a simple formula, but it works, over and over.

Today, I write four or five books each year and am published by seven different publishers in the U.S., as well as dozens of publishers in 37 languages and 53 countries. I have sold millions of books on a wide variety of subjects.

George Bernard Shaw, who became the most famous "Man of letters" in England, winning countless awards and becoming extremely wealthy, started writing at the age of twenty. But he did not sell his first work until he was 42.

For twenty-two years, he kept his job and slaved away in the evenings. When he finally began selling his works, he went on to become famous world-wide.

Harold Robbins wrote for many years before his book, "The Carpet Baggers" became a best seller, and then triggered bestselling status among all his previous books.

There are twenty steps that I have identified that anyone can follow to become an author, and then a published author.

1. Start with a message, idea, or story that you really want to share with other people. This must be something for which you have a passion, something that you believe in.

One of the best definitions of a writer is; "A person who cannot not write."

2. You must be an expert on your subject. You must know ten words for every word you write. Or the reader will know that you are talking off the top of your head.

If you want to write on success, you must already be successful. If you write on money, you must already be rich. If you write on relationships, you must be happily married.

3. Define your target market before you begin writing. Exactly who are you writing this book for?

What is the age range of the prospective reader?

What is the sex of your ideal reader?

What is the income and position of your reader?

What is the level of education of your reader?

What is his/her level of family formation?

What are the hopes, fears and dreams of your reader?
What are the desires and motivations of your reader?
What are the interests and concerns of your reader?
What are the problems that your reader has that your book will solve? What are the frustrations that your

book will take away?

For you to write a book proposal for a literary agent or for a publisher, you will have to be able to answer these questions. Otherwise, no one will consider publishing your book.

Make sure that your market is large enough. I only write books that I feel have at least one million potential book buyers.

When you write a book proposal, you will be asked to describe the type of person who will buy the book, and the number of those people that exist in the current market.

5. Buy, read and find out everything you can about other authors, books or articles dealing with the same subject. Make sure that your material is different and better than other people writing in your field in at least three ways.

6. Gather all the information that you will need to write your book. Do your research and homework before you start to write.

Paul Johnson, one of the best writers in the world today, describes how he gathers 1500 pieces of information and then organizes them from beginning to end, in a logical structure, before he begins writing a book on any subject.

To write an excellent non-fiction book, you will have to have a lot of information available to you.

7. Organize your material into seven, ten, twelve or twenty-one chapters, each following in a logical order, from beginning to end.

When I began writing, I converted my audio programs, each of which had twelve parts, into a series of twelve-chapter books.

Thinking in terms of a number of chapters forces you to decide what will be contained in each chapter, and how each of the chapters will be organized in relationship to each other.

8. Once you have a chapter title, get yourself a legal sized writing pad and jot down every key point that you could think of that could possibly be included in this chapter.

I call this the "down-dump." As you begin to write the points that should be included in this chapter, more ideas will occur to you. You will often find yourself writing two, three and four pages of material, with dozens of ideas that fall under the chapter heading.

Once you have written down all the material for each of your chapters, begin with chapter one and organize your point from the first point through to the closing part of the chapter.

9. You may want to use a "mind map" to create a visual picture of each chapter.

To do this, you take a blank sheet of paper, preferably a large sheet, and put a circle in the middle of the page. Inside this circle, you write the title of the chapter.

You then draw a line outward toward the edges of the page, and at the edge of each line draw a circle which will stand for a major subject to be covered in this page. You then draw lines out from each of these core lines upon which you write the sub-points covered under that heading.

By the time you have finished, you will have your entire chapter laid out in front of you, very much like a brain cell with ganglia connecting it to other brain cells.

10. Begin with chapter one and dictate the book in the order of the material you have chosen. Begin with your first point, a strong statement that makes a point, and arouses interest in the reader in reading further.

Dictating your book is one of the most powerful exercises I have ever discovered, and dramatically increases the speed at which you create your initial manuscript. When you dictate, you are forced to write in a conversational tone of voice. This ads warmth to your material and makes it easier and more enjoyable to read for the reader.

11. Once you have dictated the entire book, chapter by chapter, give it to a typist and have the typist type it out and give it back to you by e-mail or disk for your computer.

If for any reason you are not now using a computer for

your writing, you must begin immediately. If you have not yet learned to touch-type, immediately purchase the computer program "Mavis Beacon Teaches Typing."

By following this course, perhaps the most popular in the world, for thirty minutes each day, you will be touch typing and fluent with Microsoft Word within 60-90 days.

12. Set up a work schedule and create blocks of time consisting of two, three or four hours each. Put everything aside and discipline yourself to sit at your keyboard and edit your material during this time.

Create a space in your home or apartment. Get yourself a desk and a proper set-up. You need silence in which to work and do good editing.

13. Edit the entire book from the first word to the last word the first time. As you edit, correct the grammar and typing errors, of which there will be many. Create the necessary paragraphs, each one containing a single thought.

The first edit is the longest and the hardest job of

editing in the whole book.

14. In your second edit, break up the text with a heading every two, three or four paragraphs. This makes your writing "bite-sized" and easy to read.

15. Write an Introduction, a Preface and, if necessary, Acknowledgements for the book.

A preface explains why you are writing this book and why it is important. Sometimes you can get someone else to write the preface for you.

Your Introduction is where you explain to the reader the importance of this subject, and what he or she will gain from reading the following book.

You write your Acknowledgements if other people have helped you in the writing, the research or the publication of the book. People are very flattered to be acknowledged in a book and see their name in print.

16. In your third edit, place a quote at the beginning of each chapter. If it is a self-help or educational book of some kind, create two, three, five or even seven action steps at the end of each chapter.

When you write an action step, always begin with an imperative verb, a command.

For example, you could say "Write down three goals that you intend to accomplish within the next thirty days."

17. In your fourth edit, which will take much less time than the earlier edits, you polish the sentences, delete unnecessary material, and make final corrections.

18. In your fifth and often final edit, you completely re-read the entire book, line by line, from cover to cover. You will be amazed at the number of small mistakes that you pick up even though you have already been through the book from beginning to end four separate times.

The key to editing is that you must be satisfied with your work. You must feel that there is nothing more that you can do to improve it. Sometimes, you will have to re-write the book six or seven times, or even more.

Og Mandino, who wrote, "The Greatest Salesman in the World" and sold millions of copies once told me that he re-wrote each book thirteen to fifteen times. He said that, "My books are easy to read because they are so hard to write."

19. The entire process of writing a book as described above requires 50-100 hours of intense, focused work, after you have gathered all your material for the book.

Sometimes, the idea of writing 200-300 pages and investing more than 100 hours is overwhelming to a person. This is the reason why so many books go unwritten throughout history.

But several friends of mine, facing this dilemma, have discovered that they could go to bed early, arise early, and write one page per day. If you write one page per day, you will have a book ready to go to the publisher within twelve months.

20. Always play gentle classical music, non-vocal, in the background when you are working. Best of all, get stereo headphones and listen to classical music while you work.

What I discovered is that your brain burns out when

you write or edit for two or three hours. But when you when you wear musical headphones, you can work much longer, and when you finish you will still be alert and creative.

Getting Published

Every publishing house, large or small, is bombarded all day every day with would-be authors, striving to get the publisher to look at their manuscript.

If you go on to the website of any publishers, you will see written in big letters the instruction, "Do not mail manuscripts to our offices!"

They will not acknowledge the manuscripts, keep them, or send them back.

They will all be thrown in the trash upon arrival.

For this reason, to publish a book, you must find a literary agent. Only a literary agent can get in the door of the publisher and get a hearing. But getting a literary agent is very difficult. I have known authors who have worked for years to finally find a literary agent that was able to get them published.

To find a literary agent, go to Amazon.com and buy the books "Jeff Herman's Guide to Book Publishers," by Jeff Herman. Purchase "Guide to Literary Agents" by Chuck Sanbuchino. When you look through these books, seek a literary agent who represents the kind of book that you are writing. Literary agents usually specialize in some category whether it is romance, detective, adventure, self-help, technical, business or something else.

Another way to find a literary agent is to go to your local bookstore and open the books in the area in which you intend to write. At the front of each of these books, in the "Acknowledgements" section you will find the name of the literary agent who the author is thanking for his/her help. Write down that agents name, go onto the internet, and find out how to contact that person.

The key to getting a hearing with a literary agent, and then later with a publisher, is the book proposal. Each book proposal must contain the title of the book, an outline of the subject, a table of contents or chapter titles, and the first and second chapters that give the literary agent and/or the publisher a flavor for the quality of your writing.

Get the book, "Write the Perfect Book Proposal" by Jeff Herman, or "The Complete Idiot's Guide to Getting Published." By Sheree Buykovosky. These books will save you months and years of hard work in trying to figure out what you need to do by yourself.

To write well in any subject, you should read books on how to write well. My favorite is "On Writing Well" by William Zinnser. I also like "A Writers Time" by Kenneth Atchity. In any case, visit your local bookstore and go to the section that is full of books on how to write books written by people who have spent decades in the trade.

Finally, before you write your first book, you should purchase, "The Elements of Style" by Strunk and White. This is the gospel of good writing. It only takes an hour to read and contains about 100 one-liners that will open your mind and dramatically improve the quality of your writing.

The most important quality that you need for success as a writer, after genuine writing ability on a subject that is of interest to a large number of people, is persistence. You must be prepared to write and write and write and write, and write and write and write.

If you persist long enough and hard enough, you will eventually become a published author, and you may become one of the great writers of your generation.

Good luck!

Chapter 4

14 Tips for Writing Faster

By Kivi Leroux Miller

We all have so much content to create that we don't have the luxury of lots of time to noodle over ideas and to wordsmith to our heart's content. To succeed you have to learn to write more quickly.

Here are 14 lessons I've learned over the years in between daily blogging, writing a weekly e-newsletter, authoring two full-length books, and more.

Before You Write

Come up with a system for saving stuff you might use. I use a combination of Diigo and Evernote to save things I find online. I will forward some emails that I know I want to save for a particular use out of Gmail and into Evernote. I will take photographs of things offline, including handwritten notes, and save those to Evernote too (if I don't write too sloppily, Evernote can read my handwriting, which makes it searchable).

Sort and label as best you can as you go. I try to use a similar naming system for tagging across Diigo, Evernote, Gmail, etc. I tag based on topics, like Facebook or Writing Fast, as well as by where I might use the info, like in a Mixed Links blog post or a webinar.

Use an editorial calendar. We use a combination of a spreadsheet for the big picture and layered Google calendars for the day-to-day management.

Mind map or sketch or outline. Come up with some way to get your thoughts organized before you actually start to write. I prefer mind mapping over outlining because it helps me find the right angle or nut of the story better. Use whatever process gets you there fastest.

As You Write

Get comfortable. If you have writing traditions that get you in the mood, follow them! I always get a cup of hot tea and often a cookie. (I just ate two while writing this). I also like to be warm so I will grab a hoodie or even a blanket sometimes.

Picture whom you are writing it for in your mind. This idea (using a persona) helps you focus on the right message and choose the right words, right from the start.

Find your hook as fast as possible. I can't really get going with a piece until I know the hook. Sometimes that's the format (like this list) or sometimes it's an opinionated statement or lesson of some sort. But the faster I decide on what that is, the faster the rest of the writing goes.

Set a timer. If you get easily distracted like I do, or have a tendency to go off topic, set a timer for 10 or 15 minutes. That gives you a chance to course correct, and if you are doing great, just quickly reset it for another 15 minutes when it goes off.

Write drunk, edit sober. That's attributed to Ernest Hemingway. Self-editing as you go will really slow you down. Writing is one process, editing is another, and proofreading is yet another. Don't try to do them all at once. Give yourself the chance to write freely (since writing drunk at work isn't a great idea) before you start editing and proofreading.

Know where to find your creative genie. If you just aren't feeling it, go in search of your creative genie. I find mine most often in one of three places: when I am taking a shower, when I am walking/running, or when I am reading a book. Great ideas are more likely to come to me then compared to when I am at my desk.

After You Write

Prune it back in support of the hook. Before you start word-by-word or line editing, focus on the main point and ensuring that everything connects back to that. It doesn't make sense to start fine-tuning sentences that you may end up cutting entirely, so get the arguments or key points done first, before word smithing.

Edit what doesn't fit into a "Cut From" file. You wrote something you like, but it just doesn't work in this article. You do need to cut it, but you don't have to delete it forever. Paste it into a "Cut from" file, as in "Cut from Sally Profile." Save all that stuff in a folder so you can find it later. It's a great resource for times when you have writer's block and need somewhere to start.

Get to know your garbage. We all have bad writing habits: typos you always make, certain phrases that have become your own personal clichés. Understand that about your own writing so you can go edit it out and clean it up later.

Read it out loud and correct as you talk. Before I complete a piece, I like to read it out loud slowly -- often in a weird monotone voice that reminds me to say every single word on the screen -- with my hands on the keyboard so I can correct as I go. Reading out loud is great throughout the editing process, but I find it particularly helpful for the final proofread.

Chapter 5

Nailing a Title

By Chris E. Stout

I have had varying experiences with coming up with a title for a book. Sometimes I have had a title in mind and then built the book based on it. Other times I have struggled to get it right and to this day may wonder if I did. In other instances it is a collaborative process with the publisher or co-editor or contributing authors. The point is be open to seeing what works for your comfort level and the feedback you gain from others on the project. Also, subtitles allow you to really pitch your book to your potential reader. As you can see by this book, it was no-holds-barred. I would not do likewise for a strict academic, nonfiction book however.

For this book, I struggled with at least three others before hitting the one I went with. My process was to go to Amazon.com and search what was already published in this area/genre.

A Detailed Guide to Self-Publishing with Amazon and Other Online Booksellers: How to Print-on-Demand with CreateSpace & Make eBooks for Kindle & Other eReaders.

The Fine Print of Self-Publishing, Fourth Edition - Everything You Need to Know About the Costs, Contracts, and Process of Self-Publishing.

Self Publishing Books 101: Helping You Get Published and Noticed!

Dan Poynter's Self-Publishing Manual: How to Write, Print and Sell Your Own Book

Self-Publishing Tips and Tricks

Crush It With Kindle - How to self publish your books on Kindle and promote them to #1 bestseller status

How to Self-Publish a Book on Amazon.com: Writing, Editing, Designing, Publishing, and Marketing

From Word to Kindle: Self Publishing Your Kindle Book with Microsoft Word, or Tips for Designing and Formatting Your Text So Your Ebook Doesn't Look Horrible (Like Everyone Else's)

The Self Publishing Toolkit: How You Can Publish & Sell Kindle ebooks on Amazon

Self-Publishers Monthly

The Naked Truth About Self-Publishing

As you can see there was a lot in terms of self-publishing, and after seeing what was out there already, I came up with mine for this book.

One cool tool that I learned about is on the Lulu.com website (see: http://www.lulu.com/titlescorer) is called the TitleScorer. You just enter your working title in the field at the top of the page and use their drop-down menus to choose the variables which best describe the attributes of your title.

Then click "Analyze my title!" and you'll get a score that represents the percentage chance of its being a number one hit. Results are said to be between 9% and 83% chance of bestseller success. I'm not so sure about that, but it is fun.

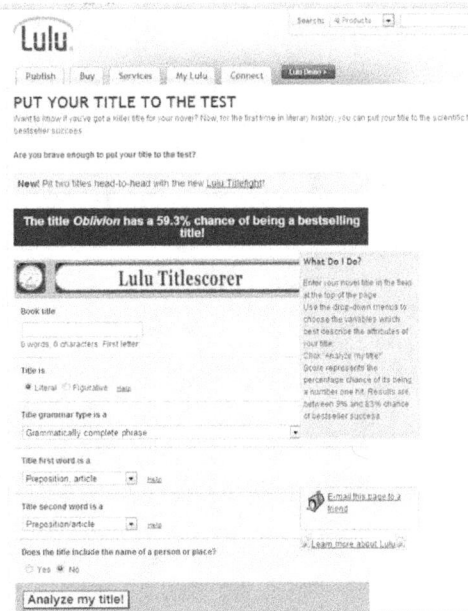

SECTION II

Economics

Chapter 6

37 Ways To Get Paid For Your Words

By Brian Feinblum

If you have great ideas, excellent writing skills, and a creative approach to your craft, you may be wondering just how you can cash-in on your genius and hard work. Well, wonder no more. Here is a list – in no set order -- of at least 37 ways to whore your wordsmith talents:

1. Advertising copywriter
2. Press kit writer
3. Website content provider

4. Write TV and radio commercials

5. Ghostwriter of books

6. Author poetry, short stories, children's books, and essays

7. Be a script doctor

8. Write catalog copy

9. Book jacket copywriter

10. Business plan writer

11. Grant writer

12. Annual reports writer

13. Technical writing

14. Paid to blog, tweet, post on FB, and other social media for others

15. Write white papers

16. Write text for educational manuals

17. Write training manuals

18. Write for business, trade, scholarly or specialized newsletters/journals

19. Co-author a book

20. Write scripts for theater, TV, film, or radio shows

21. Write book reviews or product reviews

22. Write jokes

23. Write captions for art pamphlets and photo publications
24. Articles for journals and newsletters
25. Write eulogies and obituaries
26. Speech writing
27. Write personal or corporate histories
28. Write government reports
29. Create polls, surveys, and questionnaires
30. Direct-mail copywriter
31. Brochure writer
32. Write entries for encyclopedias
33. Resume writing
34. Webinar content writing
35. Software content writing
36. Writing content for online videos
37. Self-publish a newsletter or blog for a subscription fee and/or advertising

You can also be a researcher, editor, indexer, writing consultant or writing teacher. Or maybe you can be a translator. So many possibilities! Or you can write graffiti on the walls of public restrooms – but it doesn't pay much. Other options? Write comic books, horoscopes, greeting cards, or fortune cookie sayings. Or write letters to your mom.

Of course, the best way to utilize your writing abilities is to pen the great American novel, write a great non-fiction book, and pen magazine and newspaper articles. Good luck in however you choose to apply yourself.

Brian Feinblum's views, opinions, and ideas expressed herein are his alone and not that of his employer, the nation's largest book promoter. You can follow him on Twitter @theprexpert and email him at brianfeinblum@gmail.com. He feels more important when discussed in the third-person.

Chapter 7

$0.99? $2.99? $9.99?

My Answers to eBook Pricing

Questions

By Lindsay Buroker

I went skimming through the traffic logs this morning to see what search terms people were using to find my blog and picked out a few questions related to ebook pricing. I figure if one person is asking something then others may be wondering about it too. Pricing can be a heated topic in the independent e-publishing world and almost everything in here will simply be my opinion based on my experience of the last two years, six novels, and numerous odd short stories and novellas. I hope something helps!

Ebook Pricing Q&A

How much should I charge for my novel?

As you probably already know, Amazon and many of the other retailers reward authors and publishers who create price points between $2.99 and $9.99 by offering a 70% cut of earnings. Sell for less than that or more than that and you'll only receive 35%. So a $2.99 ebook brings you a little over $2.00 whereas a $0.99 ebook only brings about 30 cents. For those who want specifics, here's a chart with the breakdown for each price point.

Anything in that $2.99 to $9.99 range is going to bring what I consider to be a decent return, per reader, for a full-length novel. At 30-60 cents, it's always felt (to me) that you can get more out of giving the novel away for free (basically using it as a loss leader to encourage sales of other books, an established and effective technique for many authors publishing series).

Of course, earnings depend on units sold, not simply earnings per unit sold, so, yes, if you can sell oodles of books at 99 cents, you can do well for yourself. That worked for some self-published authors in popular genres in 2010. This year, however, Amazon tweaked its algorithms, apparently to cut down on the numbers of 99-cent titles rocking the popularity lists. More on that in this "Updates to Amazon Book Ranking Algorithms" interview from earlier in the year.

I personally think about $5 per full-length novel is a fair price all around. It gives you far higher per-book earnings than traditionally published authors are receiving (even those whose ebooks are selling for $10+), it gives the readers a deal when compared to most traditionally published ebooks, and it's often considered a fair price by those who feel that digital books should cost less than the dead-tree variety since paper, ink, and shipping aren't a part of the equation. Lastly, it separates you from the legions of indie authors charging $0.99, $1.99, and $2.99 for their novels (often on the belief that they won't be able to sell at a higher price because they're not established names — I started out at $2.99 for just that reason). A lot of readers still walk warily around self-published books, so it can only help if you're not giving obvious clues that your book was never vetted by a gatekeeper.

How much should I charge for a short story?

For ebooks that come in under 10,000 words, authors often choose 99 cents as a price point, and I'm in agreement with that choice. Yes, you're stuck at the lower royalty rate, but a lot less work goes into writing and editing a piece that short. If reviews and sales rankings are anything to go by, readers aren't keen on the idea of $2.99 short stories, even by established authors.

But that's okay. If you sell a 100 copies a month of a 5,000-word, 99-cent story, you're still making more that year than you'd receive if you sold that same story to a pro-paying magazine. If you have a fan base established, you can sell a lot more copies than that in the first month or two you publish it. During release month, I sold about

1400 copies of my last short story (Enigma) even though I also mailed out a Smashwords coupon so readers could download it for free (and many people took advantage of that). If it follows the pattern of my other short stories, it should continue to sell 100+ copies a month. This is from a mid-list self-published author, not a best-selling indie rock star. It's why I don't bother submitting anything to magazines or anthologies any more. Even at 99 cents, you can do pretty well for the amount of work that goes into a short story.

What's up with all those free ebooks? Why would an author give away her hard work? Are these folks smoking some of that newly legal Washington pot?

I already touched on the idea of using a free ebook (a short story, a novella, or even a full-length novel) as a loss leader, the idea being that you can sell more of your other books by giving away free samples. This works particularly well with a series (and particularly less well without a series), assuming your free book is well-written, well-edited, etc. Having awesome cover art doesn't hurt either.

Another reason you'll see authors offer books for free is because they're a part of the Amazon KDP Select program (which demands exclusivity in exchange for enrolling your ebook in the Amazon Prime lending library). As a promotional perk, these authors are allowed to make their ebooks free for five days a quarter at Amazon. Receiving a pile of downloads during the free days used to help boost a book's sales ranking and visibility when it came off of the free days, though Amazon has nerfed that particular "feature" this year so that it's less effective (though not totally ineffective). There's more on that in the interview I mentioned above.

Wait, so how do you make your ebook permanently free at Amazon?

Though one never knows how long such tricks might last, you can currently make your ebook free at Barnes & Noble (through Smashwords distribution), Kobo, and iTunes, and Amazon may price-match. Here's a video I did last year to explain the free ebook/price-matching thing in more depth.

How do you make a living as an indie author?

Not exactly a question about price points, but variations of this one show up in my traffic log every day, so here's the quickie "formula."

1. Hone your craft for years, receive feedback from mentors and peers, hire an editor, and put out as rocking of a first book as you can.

2. Write many more books in the coming years (I did hit the "make a living" point about a year into this, but I had four novels and some shorter ebooks out at that point), and put something out on a regular basis (as much as we'd like to wish and hope otherwise, more books are always being published and it's rare for any one book to stay on the radar for long).

3. Promote, promote, promote. As time goes on, if you do things correctly (see next step), you'll be able to do less promoting to random people you don't know and more to your existing fans (i.e. blog, Facebook, Twitter announcements, fun extras — character interviews, cut scenes, etc.) who will then (we hope!) share news of your

work of their own accord.

4. Have a web presence (whether you need to blog or not is always up for debate — it sells some books for me directly, through the links at the right, but not a lot in the grand scheme of things) that you direct readers to (i.e. at the end of your ebook) where they can sign up for your newsletter (see my post on newsletter marketing for authors). This way, you can immediately get in touch with fans when you have a new book out. Right now, if you get a thousand purchases of your book on the day you release it, it will be enough to propel you into the Top 1000 at Amazon, something that will, at least temporarily, put you into the Top 10-20 in most sub-categories (i.e. fantasy > epic) and make you a "hot new release" in your category. Yes, this fades once sales slow down, though for some authors with books with wide appeal, this may bring the necessary attention to become a best-seller for weeks or even months on Amazon. (No, that hasn't happened with any of my stuff, but you can make a nice living simply by cultivating a core fan base and selling to them — if you haven't yet, read Kevin Kelly's 1,000 True Fans post.)

Chapter 8

Contracts a-go-go or a-no-go?

By Chris E. Stout

As discussed earlier, I've never undertaken a book project without first having a contract. You can see an actual contract I have with Wiley at https://www.slideshare.net/secret/m7UujffzyrrDvz the password: StoutOnPublishing. Keep in mind, contracts are negotiable, so if you don't see something you like, offer a counter. The key things to realize about publishing contracts in my opinion are as follow:

Advances/Royalties

The only thing better than gaining a book contract is getting the advance. Keep in mind that any advances are just that, advances. Only once your have subsequent to publication sold enough books to cover your advance, do you then begin to collect any more royalties.

Publishers vary in terms of when they pay as well. Wiley is twice a year, April and October. ABC-CILO is annually, in November. Amazon.com's CreateSpace is monthly as long as you have balances over $10. So, do read the fine print as to payment timing.

Also, the second half of your advance comes not when you send in the completed manuscript, but rather when the publisher considers it complete. Those could be two different perspectives.

Ownership

When you publish with a tradition house, you sign over copyright of your material to the publisher. You may wish to negotiate your ability to use your content on your website for instance. Generally most publishers are fine with such addendums.

Right of First Refusal

Personally, I like this clause which basically says that you as an potential author of another book must first run it by that publisher. The nice thing is now that they know you can produce, and if your new book ideas seems to have merit, they'll more readily offer you a contract. Easy-peasy. And you may be in a position to ask for a better deal on your royalty or advance. If they balk, then you are able to then consider it a refusal and take your pitch to another house.

Control and Say-So (*ha, ha*)

As a first time author, or short of a big-name, you will find that you will have little to no say in the design of the book, the physical size/dimension, paper bound or hard cover, the cover art, the font, the color of the ink, and so forth. Just know it is not you… I did have one occasion to get a sneak peek at one book's proposed cover and it was so bad that I was able to, via a supportive publisher, get alternate cover art instead.

Luddite Shocker

In a recent Wiley project I was sent an addendum to the original contract that allowed for various digital versions of the book to be made available. That was great, the more the better—Nook and Kindle here I come! But, the thing that made me feel like a geezer was that buyers could also purchase the book by-the-chapter. So, if they like chapters 5, 7, and 12, then they could buy just those chapters!

I was shocked! But then I realized that I'd been buying my music that way for years, so why not likewise for nonfiction books…?

Chapter 9

Real-World Samples of (Successful) Pitches with the Some of Big Publishing Houses

By Chris E. Stout

Wiley

The following is what Wiley sent me to respond to for my proposed book, *Getting Better at Private Practice*. You would probably see something pretty similar if you're working on a nonfiction manuscript. Following this are my responses.

If you'd like a free PDF of it go to the private link at:

https://www.slideshare.net/secret/1GFO6ZihPM9iSa and use the password: StoutOnPublishing

Wiley Proposal Guidelines

We find the following information useful, but not always essential, when considering a project for publication:

Need

Why are you developing this project? What need does it address? What developments, trends, and issues will cause the reader to want to / need to read your book?

Purpose

What is the work designed to accomplish? What kind(s) of problems does your book address and what solutions does it offer? How does it meet the need you have identified? What would the work help the practitioner or student do, understand, or improve? In what ways would the work add to current knowledge and practice?

Distinctive Selling Points

What are the distinctive selling points of your book? Are there any special materials or electronic / online components (checklists, sample forms, case studies, practice opportunities) that should be mentioned? How do they make the book clearer or more helpful?

Target Market /Audience

Please identify the primary and secondary markets for your book. If appropriate for the college market, what course would your book fit? Would your book be the central text, or one of several required readings? Does your book have any ancillaries (ex: instructor manual, power point slides, end of chapter questions, etc.) for the college market?

Table of Contents and Chapter-by-Chapter Descriptions

Provide a few sentences about the purpose and contents of each chapter, giving specific details and examples as well as general statements. Also explain the logic of the work's organization.

Knowledge Base

What is the research or experience base for the information in the project?

Title Possibilities

Along with your current working title, please suggest several alternative titles. We strive for a title that clearly communicates to all audiences the topic, purpose, and utility of a work.

Length

How many double-spaced, typewritten pages do you anticipate the manuscript to be?

Competition

What books compete most strongly with your book? If there are no direct competitive books, list those books that people are now reading that fill the need that your book will fill when published. What features make your book better?

Timetable

What schedule is envisioned for preparing the complete draft manuscript, and revisions of the manuscript? **ckground Information**

Please attach your vita, resume, or biography detailing

your professional and educational background, including prior publications.

If you'd like a free PDF of the following contents go to the private link at: https://www.slideshare.net/secret/2fvzjn6pTUl6w3 and use the password: StoutOnPublishing

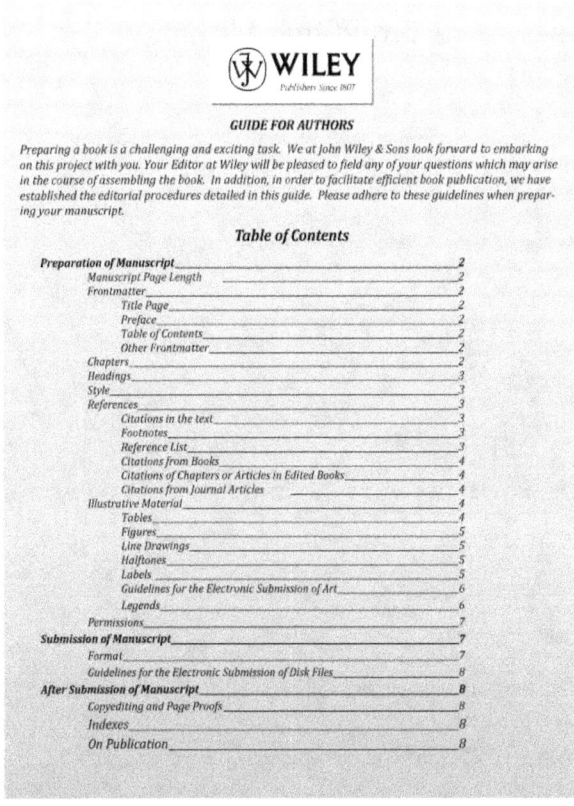

If you'd like a free PDF of **Why would someone want to buy "Getting Better at Private Practice"** the following please go to the private link at:

https://www.slideshare.net/secret/dGN04OC8N863TF

and use the password: StoutOnPublishing

On the next page is the format of what a background form looks like filled in. If you'd like a free PDF of it go to the private link at:

https://www.slideshare.net/secret/mvvGWJZaAvXG5V

and use the password: StoutOnPublishing

Greenwood Publishing

The following is what Greenwood sent me to complete for my proposed book, *The New Humanitarians.* You would probably see something pretty similar if you're working on a nonfiction manuscript for their consideration.

If you'd like a free PDF of to see what it looks like when completed, please go to the private link at: https://www.slideshare.net/secret/dmKrQG0NhyiAIO and use the password: StoutOnPublishing

The following is what Greenwood Publishing uses to evaluate your pitch. It's what's sent to peer reviewers/editorial expert consultants. Very good to know what they are looking for and help you to be sure you covered it! If you'd like a free PDF of it go to the private link at: https://www.slideshare.net/secret/2rMVF4Do3Vi6pB and use the password: StoutOnPublishing

Here is how "the story ended" with a project proposal Memo Praeger used for my book set, The New Humanitarians, which was accepted..

If you'd like a free PDF of it go to the private link at: https://www.slideshare.net/secret/vXuMeIlgr45iqz and use the password: StoutOnPublishing

Permission to Use Quote/Statement

This is the form needed to go along with a quote from person who is endorsing your new book for marketing and promotional purposes. If you'd like a free PDF of it go to the private link at:

https://www.slideshare.net/secret/dw0krCZrbe61DJ and use the password: StoutOnPublishing

May 10, 2012

Re: Permission to Use Quote/Statement

Dear [Enter Name]:

We cannot begin to express our excitement for your endorsement regarding our book, **_Getting Better at Private Practice_**. We thank you very much for your interest and enthusiasm for the book. We would like to use your comments to promote our books. We feel that using comments such as yours helps other people understand the value they shall receive from our products. If you agree that we may use your comments, please read and sign the agreement below.

This letter confirms your consent by which John Wiley & Sons, Inc. ("Wiley") and its licensees have the right and license to use (i) your personal statement, in whole or in part, in the form of a direct quote from you, and (ii) your name and address (city and state only) in connection therewith (collectively, the "Quote"). For good and valuable consideration, you hereby agree as follows:

1. You hereby grant to Wiley and its licensees the exclusive right to use the Quote.
2. The Quote may appear (i) on the front or back cover or in the front matter of any product produced by Wiley or its licensees, including in reprintings, reproductions, and/or

subsequent editions thereof, (ii) in connection with the advertising and promotion of Wiley and/or the products, and (iii) in all media in which the products may appear or be reproduced, whether now or hereafter known.

3. Wiley shall provide you with one (1) complimentary copy of the first book on which the Quote is used.

4. You hereby confirm that you are not a minor for legal consent purposes.

5. You hereby release and agree to indemnify and hold harmless Wiley and its successors, assigns and licensees from any and all claims of any kind that may be asserted against them based on its use of the Quote.

Please acknowledge your agreement with the foregoing by dating and signing this letter in the spaces provided below and returning the entire permission form to me via fax at **201-xxx-xxxx** or email to me at xxxxx@wiley.com. Please retain a copy for your records. **In addition, please be sure to include proper attribution for your quote (i.e. President, Director, Professor, author of…, etc.) on the permission form.**

Thank you very much for your interest and enthusiasm for ***Getting Better at Private Practice***. We are proud of our record of producing best-selling, high-quality products that allow our customers to learn how to do almost anything. We promise to continue this record, and hope to count you among our loyal customers for many years to come. Please feel free to contact me if you have any questions or concerns at **(201) xxx-xxxx.**

Xxxxx xxxxxxxx

John Wiley & Sons, Inc.
111 River Street, 5-01
Hoboken, NJ 07030-5774

ACKNOWLEDGED AND AGREED:

_____

Signature

_____

Date

_____

Printed Name and Title/Affiliation

_____

City, State, Zip

The Quote includes the following text: *(This is where his/her kind words about your book/work go.)*

Chris E. Stout

Chapter 10

Maybe You'll be Published In *MY* Series…?

By Chris E. Stout

Contemporary Psychology

What follows is the guide I use for soliciting interested/potential authors to pitch ME for my *Contemporary Psychology* series with Praeger (SEE: http://www.abc-clio.com/series.aspx?id=51833)

Series Information

Contemporary Psychology

Basically, I have a series with Praeger called Contemporary Psychology (see: http://www.abc-clio.com/series.aspx?id=51833) which is pretty eclectic. If you think your manuscript may be a fit, then take a look-see at the Book Proposal Guidelines below and see what you think...

We find the following information useful, but not always essential, when considering a project for publication:

Need

Why are you developing this project?

What need does it address?

What developments, trends, and issues will cause the reader to want to/need to read your book?

Purpose

What is the work designed to accomplish?

What kind(s) of problems does your book address and what solutions does it offer?

How does it meet the need you have identified?

What would the work help the practitioner or student do, understand, or improve?

In what ways would the work add to current knowledge and practice?

Distinctive Selling Points

What are the distinctive selling points of your book?

Are there any special materials or electronic/online components (checklists, sample forms, case studies, practice opportunities) that should be mentioned?

How do they make the book clearer or more helpful?

Target Market /Audience

Please identify the primary and secondary markets for your book.

If appropriate for the general interest market, what area would your book fit?

If appropriate for the professional market, what professionals would your book fit?

If appropriate for the college market, what course would your book fit?

Would your book be the central text, or one of several required readings?

Does your book have any ancillaries (ex: instructor manual, power point slides, end of chapter questions, etc.) for the college market?

Table of Contents and Chapter-by-Chapter Descriptions

Provide a draft table of contents.

Provide a few sentences about the purpose and contents of each chapter, giving specific details and examples as well as general statements.

Also explain the logic of the work's organization.

Knowledge Base

What is the research or experience base for the information in the project?

Title Possibilities

Along with your current working title, please suggest several alternative titles. We strive for a title that clearly communicates to all audiences the topic, purpose, and utility of a work.

Length

How many double-spaced, typewritten pages do you anticipate the manuscript to be?

Competition

What books compete most strongly with your book, and what are their rankings on Amazon?

If there are no direct competitive books, make the argument how you know there is a market/readers for your book.

If there are no direct competitive books, list those books that people are now reading that fill the need that your book will fill when published.

What features make your book better?

Timetable

What schedule is envisioned for preparing the complete draft manuscript, and revisions of the manuscript?

Background Information

Please attach your vita detailing your professional and educational background, including prior publications.

Please attach a biography that is supportive/relevant to your book proposal.

Don't hesitate to give me a holler if you have any questions. - CES

Chapter 11

Editor's Tools for Working with Contributing Authors

By Chris E. Stout

Wiley Contributor Agreement

The following is the Contributor Agreement for Wiley for my book *Getting Better at Private Practice*.

If you'd like a free PDF of it go to the private link at: https://www.slideshare.net/secret/2vlgsAg8qvzXVu and use the password: StoutOnPublishing

Wiley Permission Request

The following is the request form when needed permission to reprint someone else's content into your book. If you'd like a free PDF of it go to the private link at: https://www.slideshare.net/secret/7LUmKTACpqJfAw and use the password: StoutOnPublishing

---

WILEY

John Wiley & Sons, Inc.
Permissions Request

(Date)

Permissions Editor
Company Name
Street Address
City, State, and ZIP Code

Dear _____:

Chris E. Stout is editing a book in which I will have a chapter. The book, tentatively titled *Getting Better at Private Practice* to be published by John Wiley & Sons, Inc., in Spring 2012. It will be approximately 250 pages in length and will be marketed primarily to a professional audience. The Publisher also plans to publish an e-book version.

I would like your permission to reproduce the following material:

(Supply full bibliographic information for the material in question.)

I am requesting your permission to include this material in the publication mentioned above and in future hardcover, paperback, and electronic editions and revisions thereof, including the right to approve, without charge, the publication in Braille, recording, or large edition type for the visually handicapped. Because the book will be marketed internationally, we (I) must obtain nonexclusive world rights in the English language. We are (I am) also seeking rights in all languages. These rights will in no way restrict publication of your material in any other form by you or by others authorized by you. **If you do not control these rights in their entirety, please inform us (me) of the proper agency to contact.**

Below is a release form for your convenience. Please sign all three copies of this letter, return two copies to me (us), and keep the third copy for your files. Your prompt consideration of this request will be very much appreciated.

Sincerely,

_____

Author Signature

I grant permission requested on the terms stated in this letter. Credit line to be used (if different from citation given above):

_____

Agreed to and accepted: _____

Copyright Holder Signature

_____

Date

SECTION III

Self-Publishing

Chapter 12

Successful Self-Publishing

By Zepho Inc Marketing Team.

1. Product Ideas

Solve a Problem

Find a problem. People don't have the time to do their own research even though there is free information available on the Internet.

Time is money. People will pay for quick solutions. The Standard Rate & Data Service Magazine Advertising

Directory is a good place to start. This publication provides advertising information for businesses and publications.

This can be approached two different ways:

For Extrovert

Getting Started

- Find a market that interests you & explore it.

- Reach out to a few similar businesses.

- Make inquiries about their product. Keep questions open ended to invite more information.

- Request interviews.

Do Your Research

- Write down the possible issues they face: worries, challenges, and fears.

- Reorganize your list with the most important issues at the top.

- Brainstorm ideas to solve their problems simply.

- Get basic feedback. Visit epinions.com, it's one of many sites to get people's feedback and do research.

For Introvert

Getting Started

- Find a market that interests you and immerse yourself in it.

- Get a separate email address using a free online option, your ISP, or web host.

- Join online communities.

- Subscribe to every available free ezine in your market. Later, unsubscribe to the useless ones to minimize email volume.

- Subscribe to mailing lists on your subject. Be prepared for a lot of mail.

- Bookmark discussion groups related to your subject.

- Search Newsgroups focused on your topic on sites such as groups.google.com.

Do Your Research

- Read: Everything that comes in to your dedicated email account and filter as necessary.

- Think: Begin to understand the market and learn what questions people are asking the most.

- Write: Reach out to these communities and ask questions of your own – what "pain" are they dealing with?

- Create: Brainstorm ideas to solve their problems simply.

People need solutions to their problems. If you discover one issue that a market is willing to pay you to solve, you're on your way to developing a product with a strong demand.

Improve an Existing Product

Keep in mind the following simple guidelines:

- Keep what works. The strongest elements are what helped sell the work in the first place.

- Rework what doesn't. Reorganize, reconstitute, regenerate, revive – simply put, make it better.

- Add what's missing. Look at feedback about the product and consider what else can be included.

- Don't Plagiarize. Reword, paraphrase, reorganize - don't copy word for word. Be original.

The idea is to enhance the existing product. Basic elements like layout, formatting, and common knowledge can be used as a model for your improved version. This is a simple way to create a product with marketing potential.

Current trends are another avenue to explore when expanding on a proven product. If you are able to work with the right trend at the right time you can be assured to profit from the venture.

"How To" books usually do well. Focus on helping people understand software, create websites, design newsletters etc.

Here's What You Do:

- Watch for products, concepts, ideas, or a technological advancement that is popular with consumers.

- Brainstorm information products based on it.

- Develop the best idea.

- Cash in.

- Start all over again with the next big trend.

Build a business that grows with the times. Information publishing allows you the flexibility to develop multiple ideas and potentially draw in cash from a variety of revenue streams.

Reprint rights report ideas are fantastic starting points for breeding new ideas. Be wise about how to use them:

- Chose several reports, edit them, and make a new document to sell online.

- Create several documents on various reports and make your own reprint rights package.

You cannot buy the rights for an existing product and then continue to sell the exact same thing. It already saturated the market and a new trend has replaced it. Instead, cash in on the reports themselves.

Moving an existing product to another niche market is one of the simplest ways to take an idea that is already generating profit to work for you by altering it for your market.

Find a proven concept and insert your own niche or expertise:

- The Savvy _____ Guide to _____

  Ex. The Savvy Carpenter's Guide to Detailed Scrollwork

- 1001 Ways to Market Your

  _____

  Ex. 1001 Ways to Market Your Home Crafts

- Time Management for _____

  Ex. Time Management for Soccer Moms

Take the basic idea for one market and shift it to an entirely new market. Do this repeatedly. Each of these ideas can be multiplied exponentially, yet each centers on one main topic. It is the same basic idea generated for an entirely different market and completely new revenue stream.

Interchanging Ideas with Formats

Borrow someone else's success and make it your own. Take an existing, proven, information product and make your own version in a completely different format.

For Example:

- Take a great idea published in book format then create a downloadable mp3 files on the same subject.

- Take an idea from a set of videos and then create your own home-study course.

- Take a successful manual on a given topic and then develop a seminar, newsletter, instructional video, you name it.

Let's consider a collection of successful internet-based companies. You could interview between 10 - 20 owners of different successful websites via Skype, recording each with granted permission.

With an average of one hour per interview you could develop a package of mp3 files made up of separate hour long sessions. Then, you could transcribe the sessions and include the notes as bonus material or offer them linked as a more expensive premium package. You could even give them away free if orders are placed within 10 days of the launch.

The structure is : interview successful people and highlight their common product. By taking the exact same concept and changing the topic you're developing new possibilities for a great product.

Instead of interviewing website owners, you could look at professional speakers like Tony Robins, Brian Tracy, Mark Victor Hansen, and many others. The product would sell because the market is already proven with the existing product.

Getting Started:

Here are a few information product formats:

- Daily tips

- Workbook or home-study course

- Collaboration by various authors on the same topic

In addition apply the reverse concept to the above example and take a successful audio series and turn it into a video. Take the idea one step further and transcribe audio/visual materials into print resources with quality editing.

Many companies sell reprints and duplication rights to their audio/visual materials.

You won't need to generate a single new idea in order to cash in on a proven product. Also note that even if the product you're after is not available for reprint rights, ask the company anyway. You might be surprised by their answer.

If you already own the rights to a print product use it as a launching point for your own audio/visual material. Customers love choice when spending money. If the people in a given market have a compelling need to learn more about a certain subject, they will want to acquire as much information as possible in different formats.

Products Based on Non-Fiction Books & Magazine Headlines

The non-fiction books and magazines in bookstore and library are proven ideas waiting to be exploited. Magazine and book publishers labor away at producing the best possible product they can for consumers. Besides browsing physical book shelves, browse Amazon's 100 best selling non-fiction books. If a topic is there then people are willing to pay for it.

The key is adaptation and marketing. So few books

actually receive the amount of press time they deserve and disappear into oblivion. Similarly, magazines have to fight to pull in new subscribers with the best possible headlines.

Rework an information product from other people's hard work.

Book Title Examples:

From : Pet Grooming for Profit: A Complete Manual for Professional Success

To : Pet Grooming Profits: The Animal Lover's Guide to Cashing In on the Multi-Billion Dollar Pet Market

From : Ultimate Floral Arrangements: Over 150 Glorious Designs for Vases, Pots, Boxes, and Baskets

To : The 30-Minute Botanist: 201 Easy-to-Make Floral Arrangement Plans

From : How to Earn More Than $20,000 a Year with Your PC!

To : 145 Fast, Easy Ways You Can Earn $20,000 to $50,000 (or more) with Your PC

Magazine Headline Examples:

From : Seven Ways to Keep Your Kids Safe on the Streets

To : How to Keep Your Kids Out of Harm - from the Crib to College!

From : Traveling Necessities (a pet business magazine)

To : The Animal Lover's Guide to Travel

From : Horse Haggling on the Net

To : The Equestrian's Guide to the Internet

Products Based on Technology

Any new progress in technology is an avenue to reach out to consumers with an information product.

Computer Examples:

- How to profit with your computer
- How to program software for your computer
- How to become a desktop computer publisher

Internet Examples:

- How to make money online
- Where to find free stuff on the Internet
- How to surf the net

Once new technology is created, people will be looking for someone to help them use and understand it better. Watch for new advances. When something looks promising, delve into it further.

For instance, you could write an eBook user guide for software programs you have mastered. Then, when the next version of that software hits the market your same customers will be looking for the next edition of your eBook.

Don't forget, there are often products to develop with built in back ends and one-on-one consulting. Someone learning Dreamweaver is also likely to be interested in Fireworks and Flash. Many of your customers will also want the availability of personal consultation be it via Skype or phone. The possibilities are endless.

How To's & Product Information Based on Personal Interest & Expertise

Consumers want to learn how to do things. People want to be informed to save money and be able to 'do it themselves'. Any topic you can think of will likely require a step-by-step 'How to' article, guide, manual, booklet, etc. If you can tap into your personal experience and reduce extra research for a project, the time you save can be put toward the next big idea.

Topic Examples:

- How to Play the Guitar without Ever Taking a Lesson!
- How to Cook 60 Dishes - With Bacon!
- How to Buy a House - Dirt Cheap
- How to Turn Your Rubbish Into Riches!

If you need help generating ideas, flip through magazines, newspapers, or watch TV infomercials and start writing. The more ideas you create the more likely you will stumble upon a winning concept.

In addition to your own expertise in generating 'How

to' information products, your hobbies are gold mines of opportunity for making money. If you are not the expert, find someone currently profiting from the hobby and offer to interview them for an article.

Even if hobbyists do not intend to make a profit from their endeavors they will want to know everything there is to know about their hobby. If someone can turn what they do for fun into a full-time job, they will quit their current job and opt in for stress-free self-employment.

People will buy your product for the possibility of reaching their dreams. You need to focus on the desire not the necessity. The bottom line is, find a common dream and you can sell it.

What about your previous work experiences? Even if you're not comfortable developing a series of articles on The Secret Lives of Librarians you may have done your fair share of company mediating and can turn that series into How to Survive a Hostile Work Environment.

Write down a list of your:
- Interests
- Hobbies

- Collections
- Expertise
- Experiences
- Adventures
- Degrees (or educational training)
- Sports
- Businesses
- Obstacles you've overcome (turn your adversity into profits)

Use these priceless resources as a treasury for new product ideas.

When looking at your expertise consider whether it would be profitable to do a Joint Venture. If you've discovered a hot market like 'Dealing with Divorce', create an opportunity to work with an expert in the field of 'Marriage Counseling'. Take your expertise at developing eBooks and combine it with someone else's knowhow.

You make the profit from the book and your expert partner benefits on the back end with referrals to his practice.

Remember to start off with a strong sales pitch. Be sure to cover a plan for how to sell the product and what it should look like to attract your target market. Don't get into the logistics of content until the big picture is clear.

Compilations: Tips, Secrets, Ideas, Strategies, Exposed...

Organize and bring together an assortment of 'inside information' from secrets to strategies into one must-have product.

Proven Examples:

- 101 Ways To Market Your Ideas
- 999 Tested Secrets for Picking Hot Stocks
- Creativity with Found Objects - For Kids

Hot New Ideas:

- 265 No Cost/Low Cost Marketing Tips
- 55 Easy-to-Make Outfits for Your Dog
- Lost Riches! 111 Maps to Sunken Treasure!

Things to Compile:

- Recipes
- Templates

- Tips, strategies, techniques

- Reports

- Business Ideas

- Plans to build

- Patterns (for crafts and clothes)

- Secrets (Exposed!)

Now 'secrets' can be handled a couple of different ways. They can be used in a how-to capacity for revealing tips and tricks. However, people want gossip and insider information. The media is capitalizing on this trend with 'behind the scenes' stories, director commentary for movies, and the everlasting look into the lives of Hollywood stars.

Curiosity is an inherent part of humanity. The public want to know, so give them what they want - *expose a truth*.

Sample Titles:

- Insider Trading Exposed! How So Many People Have Slipped Under the Radar!

- Horse Racing Exposed! What the Experts are Not Telling You!

- Royalty Exposed! The Real Role of the Monarchy in Today's World

Compilations: Articles & Real-life Examples

Reach out to experts who have published articles in other venues. By repurposing and combining these articles in a new informative compilation you can take advantage of the fact that much of the work has already been done for you.

The same is true with practical samples, templates, and good practices. All you have to do is make contact. Call or email experts, post requests for best-practice examples and templates then build a must-have resource for your market.

Articles Compilation Example:

Say you're interested in compiling information on successful indie publishing. Access several groups dealing with the topic (i.e. authors, publishers, marketing, freelance, etc.) and post the details for your project. The next step is to request participants who've written an article on their experience and then contact those with the most promising blurbs.

Real-life Compilation Examples:

- Internet Websites
- Recipes
- Business Forms
- Art & Craft Projects
- Design Plans (home, deck, DIY Projects)
- Newsletters (newsletter formats)
- Business Plans
- Classified & Display Ads

Note: Offer a 'resource box' at the end of each article you've collected for the author to use for personal advertising in exchange for the reprint rights.

Market Directories & Pricing Guides

If you enjoy doing research, then creating a pricing guide or directory for your market could make a top information product. A directory is an assemblage of sources that reflect a particular subject.

For Example:

- If you love local tourism, create a resource of when and where to travel and with which companies.

- Enjoy a variety of winter sports? Develop a directory of the best winter playgrounds for adults and kids.

- New to the crafting market? Organize a collection of local and national hobby shows, fairs, and annual craft gatherings for purchasing supplies and selling wares.

If you're doing the research anyway and there's currently a big market or demand for your area of interest, make a directory along the way.

Examples of Current Directories:

- Family Friendly Websites
- Press Release Distribution
- Internet Yellow Pages

Popularity of these types of books is due to information overload. Consumers want a resource to make their own research simpler. Therefore the author interested in building a directory of specific resources for one particular market has the potential to make a lot of money.

Building a pricing guide for a niche market also requires a great deal of research but if you can find a market in need of such an organizational tool it can lead to a significant source of profit for your business.

Examples of Current Pricing Guides:

- Beanie Babies
- Collectable Lunch Boxes
- Antiques
- Civil War Muskets
- Pez Dispensers
- Coins

Listings in pricing guide or directory must be kept current. For directories, be aware of businesses relocating, collapsing or expanding. As this information changes, your directory will need to change with it.

Some pricing guides change as frequently as every month but if you are able to capitalize on a market that requires even a yearly update this could be your hot product.

With each update repeat customers are likely to purchase your directory again. Every update must be communicated to your clients.

Borrow Ideas from Media Talk Shows

One of the simplest ways to generate ideas for information products is by reading, listening, and watching. While we have already touched on print media as a resource, television and radio talk shows can be just as profitable.

One of the current leading talk shows focused an entire hour on people who got things for free or at a very low cost. The spectrum of guests included a man who collected gold from old computers, to a woman who found forgotten antiques at garage sales.

A self-publisher saw the merit in this program, taped it, transcribed it, retold the stories in his own words, and used them as the foundation for a marketable book.

For every show that disappears from a network line-up, new ones fill the void. It's a handy regenerative information idea pool. Consider news shows as well. Just as valuable as talk shows, the news delivers in lump-sums currently trending topics.

If it is flu season again and there's continuing

contention about the value of getting the shot. This is the time to sell product on this topic. Take advantage of the free publicity. If people are already talking about it, use that to your advantage and try to come up with unique ways of cashing in.

Some of the radio talk shows are also topic-driven. Often hosts will bring in experts and interview them. Tuning into a call-in talk radio show that permits listeners to interact with the expert allows you to judge the public interest on the topic.

How can you judge if the show is covering a hot topic? Listen for cues like the host commenting about the number of phone-lines lit up, asking the expert to stay longer, requesting the guest speaker to shorten responses to allow for more calls, callers looking for resources or a way to keep in contact with the expert. If people weren't interested in a topic, producers would not waste air-time on it.

In addition to following the show's content, often hosts will supply contact information for the expert being interviewed. Do a courtesy follow-up call after the show and see if you are able to interview the same guest for a audio product.

Updating Older Ideas

It is possible to take a marketing idea from the past and revive it. This can generally be accomplished three ways: with outdated product information packages, with books out of copyright, and with public domain government publications.

An Outdated Product Example:

Often, companies tire of their products or simply do not update their material. They do not allow for variety by publicizing the same way with the same ads year after year. But information is fluid and ever changing.

By looking through old magazines and sales letters you might come across a gem of a product like an audio package that teaches insider secrets to successful publicity campaigns. The existing product has lost its value due to old information resources. By re-recording the package on a joint venture with a local expert on marketing, you can develop an entirely new series with an initial target to the old consumer base likely looking for a fresh perspective.

An Out of Copyright Example:

When a book is no longer under copyright it becomes public domain. That's why different publishing houses are able to sell various editions of much loved classic literature like Huckleberry Finn. Focusing on non-fiction, you could uncover a guide for improving energy efficiency in your home or cottage. By adding a few chapters for new discoveries and updating phone numbers and websites you could have a hot seller on your hands eco-conscious homeowner markets.

A Government Publications Example:

Take a government publication and turn it into a new product. Use the same strategy as above but consider mixing and matching the different public domain packages you find. You could combine information on natural disasters with an army survival guide and agricultural insight on small self-sustainable farming practices as a way to prepare for and survive against the harsh changes in our global climate.

Some Places to Find Public Domain Materials:

- Agriculture
- Air Force
- Columbia
- Disasters
- Federal Emergency Management Agency
- Finance
- Library
- National Archives and Records Administration

Most Searched Keywords Online

If you knew what the hottest topics online are at any given time, you could use this information to inspire new cutting edge products.

If the top ten search terms have references to YouTube, see if this remains a hot trend for several weeks. If the additional content aligned with YouTube changes, but the keywords remain the same, you'll know immediately that videos, podcasting, and the impact of a visual medium are waiting to be exploited.

You could develop a series of best-practices on 'how to video blog' or even a guide for amateur home videographers for producing high-quality results on a low budget.

Looking at frequently searched keywords gives you an advantage for knowing what your market is hungry for. You won't have to worry about search engine optimization since the research comes built in with the knowledge of currently sought after words and phrases.

Overture's Keyword Suggestion Tool allows you to enter any keyword for an immediate search of how many people are querying that exact term or combination of words.

2. Massive Action

A List of Formats & Topics to Consider

Knowing which product formats can be offered will help bring together winning concepts for your market.

Formats

- eBook (100 pages or more)
- Booklet (Less than 100 pages)
- Book of Compiled Newsletter Issues

- Boot Camps
- Card Set (like trading cards for but for literary purposes)
- CD Transcripts
- Checklists & Forms
- Compilation of Articles from experts/authors
- Compilation of Examples (ads, press releases, etc.)
- Compilation of Secrets, Tips, Tricks, etc.
- Directory
- Guidebook (to a place or destination)
- Home Study Course on Specific Topic
- Instructional Manual (how-to)
- Posters (e.g. Government info posters for businesses)
- Pricing Guide
- Reprints Rights Package
- Seminar Transcripts
- Special Report (2 or more pages)
- Templates & Tools
- Workbook
- '_____-A-Day'(365 thoughts/tips/ideas/etc.)

Combining various formats provides your consumers with the ability to choose their preferred medium. Grouping formats around the same topic also adds perceived value to an offer. Packaging information can increase price and if done wisely, income as well.

Information Product Title Templates

Sometimes the most difficult task is not coming up with a great product idea but finding a way to make it memorable while engaging your target market. Below are various title templates and examples to help spark your imagination and stay competitive.

The Insider Secrets to _____

- The Insider Secrets to How to Be Your Own Boss
- The Insider Secrets to How to Make a Fortune with Your PC
- The Insider Secrets to How to Write a Book in 38 Days

The Truth About _____

- The Truth About Aging
- The Truth About University: 25 Lessons for Parents
- The Truth About Stingrays

How You Can _____

- How You Can Gamble with Confidence
- How You Can Golf Better Using Self-Hypnosis
- How You Can Buy from Pawn Brokers without Over Spending

The Complete Guide to _____

- The Complete Guide to Native American Baby Names
- The Complete Guide to Wildflowers
- The Complete Guide to Wild Mushrooms

_____ Made Easy

- International Border Crossings Made Easy
- Intermediate Physics Made Easy
- Entrepreneurship Made Easy

_____ Revealed!

- Alaska: A Divided State, Revealed!
- Roswell: Insider Information Revealed!
- Haggling: A Salesman's Perspective Revealed!

1001 Ways to _____

- 1001 Ways to Market Yourself
- 1001 Ways to Reignite the Romance
- 1001 Ways to Have Fun with Paper

How to _____

- How to Be Your Own Boss
- How to Cook With Curry
- How to Identify Edible Wild Berries

The Ultimate Guide to _____

- The Ultimate Guide to Tutoring
- The Ultimate Guide to Writing Contests
- The Ultimate Guide to Understanding Organic Foods

_____ Exposed!

- Travel Health Care Exposed!
- The Real Nazi Furor Exposed!
- Hollywood Casting: The 'Ins & Outs' of Playing Your Part Exposed!

The Truth Behind _____

- Have We Been Visited: The Truth Behind UFO Conspiracy Theories
- The Truth Behind The Super-virus
- Marauders: The Truth Behind Lost & Buried Treasure

The Art of _____

- The Art of Spirit Walks
- The Art of Speech Writing
- The Art of Casual Conversation

The _____ 's Guide to _____

- The Girl's Guide to Wilderness Survival
- The Complete Idiot's Guide to Understanding Real Estate
- The Absolute Beginner's Guide to Babysitting

Use A Specific Number in Your Title

- 14 Habits to Avoid in Public

- 25 Unique Weddings – and How to Craft Your Own

- 501 Questions Every Parent Should Know How to Answer

Mix and match templates to develop new information product ideas.

For Example:

- **The Naked Truth About Skin Cancer**

By inserting a descriptive word before 'Truth' that

relates to and plays on the remainder of your topic you are inherently building in a memorable link for readers.

- **18 Little--Known Secrets to Winning Arguments**

  By adding a concrete number to the beginning and changing 'Insider' to 'Little-Known' you add both the promise of various secrets to the lure of potentially new information aimed at a general readership that 'Insider' may alienate due to the formality of the word.

- **The Art of Soufflés - Made Easy!**

  By combining the idea of 'Art,' or something that requires a lot of work to achieve, with the concept of relative ease allows potential buyers to believe that the unattainable might just be manageable.

Creating a Tips Booklet

Developing the right 'free' tips booklet can draw a wide variety of consumers in your niche market to your website. People want fast, reliable information that's easy to read and can be instantly applied.

Marketing a tips booklet is one of the best

opportunities for publicity. By making your booklet a free-downloadable item, your competition is likely to scoop it up and make it available on their websites too. They are advertising your expertise for free.

With any tips booklet the key is in the title: 88 Ways To-, 745 Easy Designs For-, 156 Golf Tips to Improve Your Score, and 101 Quick Meal Ideas. One of the top selling tips books is '1001 Ways to Be Romantic.' and what did author Gregory Godek do? He developed a sequel, '1001 More Ways to Be Romantic.' This is an attainable and realistic goal.

What to Do:

- Devote a notebook to your idea.
- Jot down all the points already mulling around in your head.
- Under each tip write a simple explanatory paragraph.
- Close the book, but always keep it nearby

The last point is crucial since the task should not be a taxing one. Whenever you think of another idea to add to your list, write it down. If you are out living your life, make use of your time and don't wait to write a sudden idea down. Those are the best ones likely to be forgotten. Ask for people to send you ideas from the mailing lists, forums, and groups. Utilize your resources and optimize your down time.

Interviews

Producing a book based on expert advice is a great way to reduce time spent on research.

Finding Experts

Always know in advance what your final product will be. If your intent is an eBook only, you can look at phone, Skype and email interviews. The experts you contact need to know in advance if their voice or image will be recorded. Search for experts online, in magazines, as authors of books on the subject, or college professors. Make two lists: Preferred and Back Up.

Contact experts on your preferred list by phone, mail, or email. Many experts do not answer their own email and this is likely to be a long shot. Due to time constraints or nerves about being recorded, some may not be able to commit to the project. Use your backup list to fill any gaps.

Usually highlighting their achievements and current projects in a resource box or via a well-placed question is sufficient return for their investment, but occasionally an expert will charge a small fee. Pay it if he is a key expert for your market. It will be worth it.

Developing Questions

Questioning is the key to a good interview. Avoid closed-ended questions like, 'Did you have a particular market in mind when you developed this product?' Use open-ended questions like, 'Could you describe your initial reactions when you first developed this product?' These will coax out interesting tidbits in conversation.

Question Prompts to Guide You:

- Could you describe...
- Can you tell me about...
- What is the story behind...
- What is the difference between...
- Can you elaborate on...
- How were you able to...

The words in bold above invite discussion and detailed responses. It will take time to develop the skill for creating engaging questions, but by watching other interviews on radio or TV you will pick up on points such as Lead Ups and Follow Ups.

A Lead Up is information supplied by you that the guest may not be aware of for which you base your next question around. Follow Ups are remarks or brief questions to further draw out information regarding the question asked. However, knowing the definition of these terms is not the same as practicing and honing the skill.

If you choose to do email interviews Follow Ups or responses to statements are difficult to incorporate. Likely you will need advance approval to address such ideas in a reply email. If a guest agrees, you will probably only get one more chance to refine the content.

Being Prepared

Keep your interview focused on the wants and needs of your target market. If you have done your research then your questions will naturally flow around what your audience wants to know. If this is a topic you truly enjoy, it will be easy to keep the interview interesting by allowing your passion to engage your guest and set the tone. Interviews are basically built around a conversation you want to have in the first place.

Make sure to prepare your list of questions ahead of time. It is common courtesy to send your guest what you intend to ask at least 24 hrs in advance, but 3-5 days prior is preferred. This will allow for familiarity with the content and usually produces a more fluid and relaxed interview.

Don't include all the questions you hope to ask, you will never be certain which Follow Ups you might need until the interview is happening. Make the list of topics and the main focus questions available to the guest. Have your list of questions with you during the live interview. It is important that both of you are prepared and at ease.

When doing a phone interview, make sure there is good connection on both ends and audio recording equipment has been tested.

If you have chosen to Skype your interview you will need an external recording device either audio/video capable or audio specific. Once a recording is complete you need to edit, either for sound quality or to maintain consistency with the length of each interview.

Article Compilation

Reach out to various experts in two different ways: ask if they have an article available for reprint that follows your topic, or request reprint rights to an article you already have in mind. Don't forget to provide room for a resource box to allow contributors to be contacted by future readers.

Once you have the articles you require, compose a brief introduction about the collection and its impact on your niche market. Arrange the articles into a logical format for your book. Create a table of contents and you are ready to go.

Resource Guide, Pricing Schedule, or Rolodex Style

Compiling resources in an easy-to-use format on a particular field can be valuable to readers. Most people don't want to spend their time looking for one particular resource. By collecting the most useful resources for a niche market you can make money by making other people's lives easier.

The top selling 'Net Detective' is a resource compiled of thousands of web site links for finding people and performing background checks. This is a massive list of private investigation links. Keep your content simple but valuable.

Compiling a brief annotated bibliography for each of your resources can have enormous benefit to your consumers. People don't like wasting time and want to be competitive. Simply determine who needs a tool-box of information resources.

Online search for template examples will provide you with a variety of formatting options for your product.

A Few Resources to Consider:

- web sites/blogs
- contact numbers/email
- regional/global listings
- templates/forms
- samples/examples/designs
- books
- audio/visual/media
- images
- articles

- model numbers

Buying Reprint Rights, Licensing

When you have found the right product with reprint rights available, buy the onetime reprint rights fee and you are able to sell without paying royalties on it. Be certain that you have the right to distribute digitally: eBook, CD, CD-ROM, video, audio, etc. Occasionally the rights to print and digital are separated due to an already filled request or a joint venture where the rights were divided.

Finding the right reprints can be a challenge and you need to stay alert for when they are offered. You can offer to buy existing rights for a self-published product. It is difficult to buy reprints from a traditional publisher. You won't know the answer until you ask the question. Be prepared to hear a lot of "No's" but don't let it get you down. At some point, someone will say "Yes."

Ask questions and know your rights before you consider purchasing any reprint, no matter how promising they appear.

Project Planning

Planning and organizing the scope of your project will make a large venture manageable. To write a book, create an outline of the contents. Then focus on writing an article about each sub-heading or chapter you have included on your outline. By breaking the work down into smaller sections, it is easier to think and write.

Basic Outline Template:

Introduction

- General sales pitch or "hook"
- A simple or broad description of the overall contents
- Key points to look for in the subheadings to follow

Main Body

- One heading for each idea/article
- A few points listed below each heading to remind yourself what you want to focus on
- What understanding or insight readers should leave with
- The most important points to remember and things to follow through on
- Any references or contact information

Don't be overwhelmed by the enormity of a project. Taking control of your idea and setting attainable short-term goals will make the work less daunting and allow you to take action.

Consider breaking up your sub-headings into per-page ideas. Writing about each idea in depth, without the distractions of the rest of the chapter, will allow your mind to relax and be more productive.

This strategy will benefit you twofold: not only will it make setting and achieving goals realistic and attainable, but it will highlight and focus your thoughts for readers as well. People don't have the time to muddle through vast chunks of words looking for the information they need. By being concise with a separate focus for each page, readers can easily navigate and your book becomes a useful tool.

When you are developing a project on a larger scale, the first few weeks should be spent brainstorming lists of topics, chapters, headings, sub-headings, side notes, etc. After organizing the results into a cohesive table of contents, set your attainable writing goals for each day and week until you have finished the project.

It is important not to overload your daily schedule. Plan in down-time to avoid those lazy-days where you just don't want to work on anything. If your goal is to write every morning and save the afternoon for relaxing, stick to the plan. Once you get into a rut and begin avoiding the project, it will be more difficult to recommit yourself as time passes. Don't give yourself an excuse to put it off to another day.

Hiring Ghostwriters & Freelancers

Whether a project is too big for you to tackle alone or you just don't have the time to adequately devote to the developmental stage, hiring a ghostwriter may be worth your budget.

In addition to hiring ghostwriters, freelance workers can be used for any and all stages of your product development: researching, transcribing, editing, writing, recording, etc. Decide how much time you can commit to the project and the budget you have for contracting out the remaining work.

A good but unknown writer can be hired for $1000 - $2000 for a full-length book developed from your research.

Many of the novels attributed to established political figures, movie stars, and athletes are really written by ghostwriters.

How to Find Ghostwriters & Freelancers:

- Call your local newspaper office and make inquiries.
- Go to the public library and get a publication called Literary Marketplace.
- Run an ad in the paper.
- Elance

Working with the writers and freelancers is a time saver. After posting the details of your project, service providers bid on your job. You can review portfolios, look at references, and ask questions on private discussion boards before hiring.

3. Guidelines

Managing Ideas

It's now time to manage your data and build an idea file. Most of the suggestions for developing winning product are based on developing various types of preexisting media. You can scan and save your findings or maintain a paper file folder.

Be Sure to Collect:

- Newspaper & magazine clippings
- Book reviews
- Sales letters for hot information products
- Display ads for hot information products
- Information product titles
- Samples of chapter headings, layouts, etc.

Waiting for that one big original idea would be a slow road to travel. Using the concepts offered in this book will help you generate and follow through with multiple ideas. In turn, you will discover your one 'money maker' - your diamond in the rough.

Place all sources you find to help fuel your ideas in the folder. Periodically reevaluate this file to reorganize current hot topics and discard items that no longer hold impact. Give yourself the freedom to explore opportunities and you will automatically begin to reorganize and refocus the way you think.

Often mental blocks happen and this file can help. Not all of your ideas will be winners. Keep everything, you never know when a thought will spark something better at a later glance. When your ideas flow freely, capture everything.

However, there will be times when you are stuck and you can't generate anything new. Don't let it get you down. Here are a few things you can do to get motivated again:

Play What If:

Simply ask yourself, "What if I ...(did this instead of that)?". Change your formatting around for different ideas.

- What if I used the booklet as the lure to get them to buy my bigger course?
- What if instead of writing it, I put it on a mp3?

Use Creative Thinking Books:

Below is a list of renowned books ideal for breaking any slump:

- A Whack on the Side of the Head: How you Can be More Creative! By Roger von Oech

- A Kick in the Seat of the Pants By Roger von Oech

- Get Out of Your Thinking Box By Lindsay Collier

- Five Star Mind: Games & Exercises to Stimulate Your Creativity & Imagination By Tom Wujec

The time spent on generating the best possible ideas will help you maximize your profits.

Create Your Product with Laser Focus

Part of the development stage is narrowing down your focus to a handful of projects from the wide variety of ideas.

Ask Yourself:

- What do people always ask you about?
- Do you have special knowledge others would like to know?
- Have you experienced certain setbacks in life and overcome them?
- Have you succeeded in a career that many people fail at?
- What subjects interest you the most?
- What jobs have you held?
- What skills do you have?

Having more than one answer per question is natural. Now ask five closest friends or relatives the same questions. By comparing your answers to your friends' answers and prioritizing your findings, you will further narrow down to one answer for each question and hone in on the best possibilities you generated in your idea file. Choose one idea.

Before diving into Project Planning, there is still a bit of ground work to do. You need to get your ideas organized before dividing them into workable chunks. Take time to brainstorm on paper.

Mind Mapping helps to organize and clarify your thoughts. By visually linking words and ideas to your main theme you can classify, problem solve, and make decisions that will set the ground work for your Project Planning.

Mind Mapping:

- Write your product idea in a box in the middle of the page. e.g. How to be a Magician for Fun & Profit
- Branch off with evenly spaced lines around your box to highlight main points to cover. e.g. Techniques / Rolodex / Marketing Your Persona / Learning from Experts

- Create as many sub-branches as you need to narrow in on the specifics of those main points. e.g. Techniques: Your Character / Choosing a Name / Tricks
- Continue to branch out with specific ideas to round out each sub-point e.g. Tricks: Rabbit in Hat / Pick a Card / Flowers from Wand / Coin Behind Ear / etc.

Imagine the bonuses to help sell your product. List them in a blank space on your map page. Typically the upper left corner is a good spot for the expansion of additional ideas. For an eBook, here are potential bonuses:

- Interviews of successful magicians
- Copies of letter, ads, and postcards successfully used to get work
- Million-dollar Rolodex of suppliers and talent agencies

Other irresistible offers:

- eBooks: There are hundreds of eBooks with free redistribution rights. Search for "free e-books."
- Articles: It is not uncommon for people to give articles away for extra publicity. Collect them into a free bonus.
- Your own tools. As you work through various projects you create templates and compile research that others consider highly valuable.
- Other public domain material.

- Licensed products, reports, etc.
- Free reports
- Other people's products or services.
- Discount coupons towards a service or product.
- Free reprint/resale rights

Sample Email for Querying Use of Free Material:

Hello,

My name is _____ and I'm republishing a book on color pallets famous artists have used. (The site is not yet up.)

I found your program the other day from download.com and I'd love to include your product as a free bonus to anyone who orders my eBook. As per your license agreement, I am emailing to request permission. I can direct people to the download.com site here: (insert active link) so they will always get the latest version.

I really appreciate the opportunity to help get the word out about this fabulous program.

Please let me know if this is okay with you.

Thank you,

(Your Name or Auto Signature)

(Your email address)

(A phone number to contact you at)

As you begin to work with your product idea remember that simplicity is the key. A one page web site will typically make more money than a multi-page site.

Don't be afraid to fail. It will happen to some of your ideas. Accept and learn from it. You will also have a lot of winners.

Finally, if you don't know something don't feel like you have to learn it. Utilize outside resources for helping you get your product launched faster.

Follow the Footsteps of Successful Businesses

It is not necessary to start from scratch when building your business. In fact, it is labor-some. The best advice to make headway on your business is to borrow what already works.

This is called modeling. If you get bogged down developing a plan from ground up, you might give up on it.

Here's What You Do:

- Find a business you admire

- Study its business model and practices

- Use that information as a framework for your own business

- Tweak the product idea to make it your own or use an idea you have already to round out the plan

- Develop your business strategy using a similar platform. When the bulk of the work has already been done for you by someone else, use it as a resource.

Start with a fast and simple project to give yourself the experience and confidence to build the bigger ideas. Smaller projects that vary in formatting will provide you with opportunities to build your own template resources. Then, when you develop your grand ideas, you have the advice from above to work along with your own personal experience.

Don't get too excited about any one project you're working on. If you realize the idea won't be an easy sell, set it aside to revisit another time. Get your feet wet with high-interest products that are fast and easy to set up.

Do Your Homework

Before you commit yourself to an idea, research your market. Understanding your niche market will help you narrow down your ideas to the best possible product and avoid losing time on weaker projects that don't fulfill a desire. If you are not familiar with your target market then follow these guidelines:

Money

Your prospective customers must have disposable income. You need to make sure they have the money to spend on your idea.

Reachable

The accessibility of your market is important in being able to show them what they need. Visit frequently trafficked websites, ezines, and popular blogs. Consider the cost-effectiveness to advertise or do a joint-venture with high-traffic sites. Utilize groups.google.com to look through newsgroups and forums to discover where your target audience visits often.

Online

If your consumers are not online then selling them an online, digitally delivered product does not make sense.

Survey

Continue your research using search engines. Find discussion boards and lists for your market: type "your market + discussion board." Visit these sites and read.

Get involved with the conversation and discover what is needed. You could also rent a mailing list of buyers in your target market. The feedback you get will allow you to tweak your idea to what is currently relevant.

Competition

Research your competition. Don't worry if there is already a similar product available. Be glad. Take the time to analyze what they offer and how you can modify, improve, or spin your idea in a different way. If a particular company has been in business for a while, take the time to act as a prospective buyer to learn more about their marketing techniques. While it may appear on the surface that they offer the same product for a low price, it may only be a launching point for their business model. Once a consumer is hooked, a company may have various other products they offer at increasingly higher rates that contribute to their overall sales. You need to understand your competition in order to make their marketing strategies work for you.

Marketing

After studying your competition you should have a good sense about what consumers like to buy. Give them what they want. Let this information help you weed out the weaker ideas and pare down this area of your idea file.

Joint-venture

Make the market work for you by having it work with you. Consider joining forces with a pre-existing high-traffic website that is not capitalizing on your product idea. If you can use someone else's hard earned consumer base and sell them on your idea, you can save yourself a lot of time and effort. On the other hand, tagteaming with an existing site where you each link to the other's web page is another way to get the competition working for you instead of against you.

Test Your Product

You need an effective plan to test product ideas on your markets within weeks or even days. The goal is to find the most profitable idea for your target market.

The amount of money spent on marketing your product does not directly translate into profits. You need to save valuable time for potential winning ideas. Learn how to reduce the risk of pouring money into an unsuccessful idea. Find ways to test products faster in order to find the right one.

Pre-Publication Offer

A pre-publication offer is selling your product before you finish it. Dry-testing is discouraged by the Federal Trade Commission because consumers buy believing the product is ready. However, selling your product before it's complete will give you excellent feedback about its marketability.

A Pre-publication offer makes it clearly known to buyers that the product is still being developed with an expected publication date. If very little response is generated for your idea, simply return the money from any orders you do receive.

This approach can be risky. If you decide to move forward with the product you need to avoid buyer's remorse. The best way to avoid buyer's remorse is to keep your customers updated on your progress. In addition, offer them a free gift or bonus when pre-orders come in. That way, your customers are both informed and have something in their hands to fuel their interest in the coming product.

When using the pre-publication method, you might be worried about how long it will take to manufacture your product. Consider a joint-venture with a company selling a similar product. Begin filling orders with the other product as a hold-over. Then when you are ready, send all of your customers the long awaited pre-purchased product you've been working on.

No matter what, keep the lines of communication open with your customers. If they feel like you've abandoned them, they will abandon you.

Free Publicity Testing

Develop and launch a press release. Media outlets know what their consumers want and if your idea is picked up and talked about, you know you have a winning product. If public response is flat or nonexistent you know to abandon that idea and move on to the next.

Market Your Options

If you have a number of product ideas to consider, let your niche market decide which one to follow through on. Write a series of small reports, 3-5 pages in length. Reveal a sampling of what the larger product would cover. Don't give away all the best information in these reports, just a few of the many details contained in your idea. Reach out to your target market and let them know about your reports.

Utilize your current customers:

- Send them a list of your entire selection of reports
- Let them pick 3 to get for free
- Keep track of which report is requested the most
  This continues to build relationship with your existing

customers while gathering important information about which of your ideas is most valuable. By letting consumers choose, they feel empowered and in control. This will provide you with happy customers and a reliable free way to test the market.

Reach out to your target market:

If you are first into a particular market where you don't have a customer base.

Don't worry. Your goal may be a little difficult to achieve but it can be managed by either selling your reports or giving them away.

Options for reaching your market:

- Consider a joint-venture with a company to have them include the report list & contact information to put in outgoing packages.
- Develop a website that offers each report with online ordering using a secured server.
- Set up a website for unlimited free downloads & track numbers using a generic statistic system.

You are likely to get a higher response by offering a free choice with the above options. Your goal is to see what the market wants before you spend the time in development.

Once you have narrowed down your focus to one marketable idea, there is more testing to be done. You need to consider other variables such as your pricing, your guarantee, and mailing lists.

Don't fall into the trap of thinking your idea is perfect just as you imagined it.

Test, test, test. Only after you have confirmed beyond a doubt that your idea will sell big do you move on to the next phase of development.

Testing with Multiple Landing Pages

The expert marketers don't sell their products directly through a sales letter. They use 'soft-sell' content pieces to build a relationship with a prospective customer before giving them the big sales pitch.

This approach is great for the affiliates because they don't have to spend a lot of time 'warming-up' their audiences before sending them to the marketer's website. They just have to point to the awesome new freebie that has been released and let the expert marketer do the selling.

It would be great to let your affiliates refer their audience to free videos, special reports, webinars, etc. when they promote your product rather than sending them straight to a sales pitch. Click Plan allows you to :

- Create multiple landing pages for a product
- Create customized landing pages for special Joint Venture promotions, free report etc.
- Let affiliates promote a post on your blog or any of your freebies

You can send your hoplink to your product sales page or any of the landing pages you set up. This allows your affiliates choose the best way to promote to their audience.

Pricing

There is a balance between the uniqueness of a product in a particular market and perceived value of that product by consumers. Don't sell yourself short: undercutting the competition will not always bring a higher volume of sales. Depending on your target market, a lesser priced offer may prevent sales due to perceived value – it's not as good as all the others and that's why it costs less.

You need to research what is already being offered and for how much. Also, consider the value of your product to your market. If what you're offering allows someone the potential to make an extra $5000, you could price your product between $100 - $200, right? Not necessarily. You need to consider if your niche market is more hobby-related or not. It is more realistic to sell a digital product between $14.95 and $19.95 to hobbyists.

Test different price points. In a case study looking at online sales of a new psychiatric based book, a three day test was conducted with varying price points: $7.95, $14.00, and $24.95. While profits were initially higher with the book priced at $24.95, more customers were reached with at $14.00. Over an extended period time, the marginal difference in total profit between the two competing price ranges would not be significant enough to choose the higher price. Overall, the greater customer base generated at $14.00 is advantageous for the development of a long term clientele.

Just remember, the more unique and specialized your information is, the more you can charge for it.

Publicity

- We have touched on a variety of different mediums for getting out your message:
- Direct Mailing (your own list or rent a list)
- Joint-venture with an established high-traffic website or business
- Online Social Media Groups, newsgroups, forums, & blogs
- Press releases
- Traditional advertising in print, online, on TV, or on the radio

We have even looked at sure-fire formulas and templates for titles:

- How to's
- Survival Guides
- Exposed!
- Tips & Secrets
- 1001 Ways

In the end it will be your headline that sells your product. Title has to be the right one for your product. You need to draw in your target market with the right words in the right order to entice them to learn more. Be sure to answer these questions for your intended audience:

- So what?
- Who cares?
- What's in it for me?
- Why are you bothering me?

If your title can highlight the answers to these questions then you are starting off on the right foot.

In addition to your headline, any bullet points you use in the sale of your product are key for your advertising. Each bullet point is a mini-headline. Having just one compelling bullet that a consumer is interested in can turn the sale to your favor. Focus on revealing your best secrets with each point. People don't want to read an essay to see if they want what you're offering. Your goal should be to arouse curiosity and confirm the desire for your product.

A chunk of copy on the screen will be bypassed instantly. Concise, well spaced and balanced mini-headlines will draw a reader's eye by making the copy look easy to read.

Below are some helpful bullet formulas. The

underlined areas are the "fill in the blank spots:"

  -*Six* of the top-selling products on the _____

and why.

- How to turn $XXX into $X,XXX in less than 14 days with _____.
- How a _____ got 200 new customers in nine days.
- The amazing secret of getting new customers for you business.
- How to revive a dead car battery without jumper cables.
- Stop _____ without expensive_____.
- Quick and easy_____.
- Five simple ways to _____.
- The secret of _____.

  The key is to highlight the best your product has to offer. In doing so, your headlines and descriptive bullets will publicize your product more efficiently. Consider what elements will work best for your budget, product, and your market. You will have a winning product.

Managing Your Expectations

  Be realistic as you explore the possibilities in self-publishing. Nobody starts off as an expert. You need to have a mental strategy to balance out your *statistical* strategy.

Your expectations determine your results. Maintaining a positive frame of mind is necessary. You also need to know your market inside and out. Becoming an expert in your field only takes an hour of reading, studying, or listening a day. Immerse yourself in knowledge to have the understanding and realistic positive expectancy about the product you are going to launch.

Be proactive as you work toward your goals. Don't overwhelm yourself with the big picture. Prioritize and focus on one task each day. It may not feel like you're getting anywhere but with each new day and each new item tackled, momentum will build and progress will become tangible.

Don't miss a single day. If you allow yourself to miss even one day working on your project, it will rapidly gain momentum. Before you know it a week will go by and you've done nothing.

Remember the 80/20 rule: 20 percent of your actions produce 80 percent of your results, whereas nothing begets nothing. Compelling yourself to complete one task a day on "important but not urgent" items from your to do list will keep you actively working toward your final goal.

Find Support Join your local writer's meetups to share and learn from successful writers. It will provide support to accomplish your goals. Find a mentor who can help you overcome obstacles.

Decision making is a skill you will need to develop if it doesn't come naturally to you. Often it is the finality of a decision made, that closing of options and doors that makes people nervous. Don't stop your progress. In order to get your product developed, you will need to narrow your scope and focus on what is relevant in that moment for your particular market.

Keep moving forward. Once you have committed yourself to an idea, opportunities will present themselves. Making a decision is not a lost avenue but an opportunity found.

Deadliness are important time management tools. If you never set a deadline for yourself, you will be hard pressed to finish anything. Your goal is to launch your product. When? What is a realistic timeline?

You need to make yourself accountable. Without a clear deadline, there is always one more thing to add or edit to complete. Confide your plans in the right friend. By sharing your end-game you will motivate yourself on a whole new level. Plans come together and avenues open up when you focus on an attainable goal. You will find a way to meet your deadlines and feel the pride that goes along with doing a job well.

Our choices are what make us great. Take action and you take control of your destiny. If you waste time then you are taking valuable time away from your project. By choosing to read a book on your niche market, scanning the net for resources, or talking to experts equates to one or more tasks completed each day toward your goal.

Balancing your day job, family life, social life, and free time with the intent to create a hot information product is not easy. Don't try to keep everything up in your head or on the tiny screen of your daily planner.

Schedule a week's worth of time for yourself, including meal breaks and down time on a full sheet of paper. If your personal time out-weighs time spent on your project, do some recalculation. Then try it out for two weeks. By the end of the second week you should no longer need to refer to a schedule - you'll know the rhythm of your day. It's crucial to identify on the page or screen what you intend to accomplish. Combine this information with your project outline and completing one or more tasks a day suddenly becomes second nature.

A word of caution about projects and goals: don't take too much on at once. You may be thinking that if you can develop 10 projects that pull in $1,000 each a month, you'll make $10,000 every month. As nice a thought as that is, it's easy to become sidetracked and lose focus. Keep it simple. Concentrate on one idea at a time. Focus all of your energy into that one product and make it shine. Only after a successful launch for that first project should you look at the next one.

Take it one step at a time, one task each day, and one product competently developed. Soon you will develop strong work habits to build a successful self-publishing business.

Author's Note: Licensed under the Creative Commons License, Attribution 2.5.

About Click Plan

Click Plan is a product of Zepho Inc, founded by Bala Paranj. He completed his MS in Electrical Engineering from Wichita State University. He has self published software development books. Over a period of 10 years he has used many software solutions for self publishers.However, he became frustrated with the existing solutions. He decided to develop a software as a service product to help self publishers succeed. You can signup for a free two week trial at www.clickplan.net. You can contact him by email at support@zepho.com.

Chapter 13

How to Blog Daily

By Kivi Leroux Miller

I've been blogging Monday – Friday (or darn close) for about 18 months now. It's not easy, but it's worth it.

Here are a few tips based on what I've learned along the way:

Sketch out an editorial calendar. Even if you don't follow it exactly (and I rarely do), it helps you keep on track with the kinds of things you want your blog to be known for.

Get help from guest bloggers. We try to publish a guest post about once a week. It takes some of the pressure off and freshens up the voice.

Come up with some regular features. We publish Mixed Links, a round-up post at least every other Friday. I'm thinking about coming up with some other standing features too. It's one less post you have to get creative with and it creates things for readers to look forward to.

Get help with the blog admin. Kristina manages our guest posting schedule, formats the guests posts, and creates the first draft of Mixed Links. She also does a fair number of first drafts for me (e.g., when we summarize a report), and sometimes guest posts herself.

Make room to go with what strikes you. The easiest posts to write are the ones that you are emotional about in some way, whether it's excited, or impressed, or annoyed. When the mood strikes, scrap what's scheduled and write it!

Make it a habit. I'll often post late in the day (it's after

4 pm now), but I'm nearly religious about getting something up on the blog, even if it is a little later than I'd hoped. Here's how Katya Andresen describes her daily blogging habit:

> Around 10 or 11 pm the night before I schedule a post to be published, I sit down and reflect on what meaningful thing I heard, read or thought during the day, and I write about it. It's that simple and that hard.

Write ahead. When I get a break, or when I know I am going to be traveling a lot, I'll try to write several posts in advance of when I actually publish them. I can always bump them to a later date if something really timely comes up.

When in doubt, do a list post!.

Chapter 14

My Approach to Blogging

By Chris E Stout

I was fortunate to become part of LinkedIn's Influencers (see: http://www.linkedin.com/influencer/3055695) and it has been a great experience. While they have an editorial calendar with monthly topical points, you are not bound to write to that. I feel that I am still learning the ropes with it, and it is an interesting experiment to see what gains a high number of views or comments. It is a good tool to also get one's name or work "out there" as well.

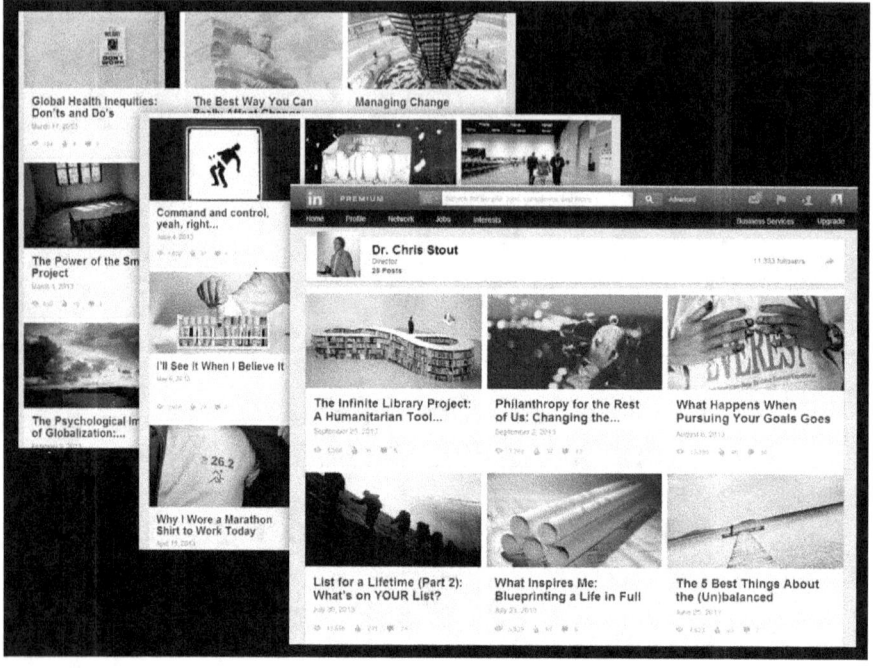

Chapter 15

Thoughts and Warnings on Self-Publishing

By Chris E Stout

First of all, there are a number (and growing) ways to self-publish. Historically there were places not kindly known as "vanity publishers" who were really glorified printers that had a reputation of printing/publishing almost anything as long as it was paid for by the author. The content usually was a vanity autobiography or something that otherwise no reputable publishing house would touch.

Today, technology has changed this. Indeed, the expectation from traditional publishing houses for authors to promote their own books, establish their own websites, etcetera, while still paying so little a royalty has lead to the advent of CreateSpace and others that offer more to the authors.

First the Warnings

If you are considering a service to self-publish, be aware that they frequently overcharge for what they do versus other sites using a different model. They may try to up-sell you services you do not need (for example, ISBNs are free, or expensive promotional packages). They may over promise what they do for you. You could be hoodwinked into purchasing a garage full of books that will rot before they sell.

So, first consider what you need, what you are able and willing to do yourself, and what you can afford. Then "comparison shop." Here is a site that does so for the Top 10 such companies: http://online-book-publishing-review.toptenreviews.com /

Chapter 16

Print on Demand

By Chris E Stout

Blurb

I have used Blurb for my non-profit to do a picture book as a donor-thank-you gift. back when they still had Blurb-for-Good. I like them. Their ease of use was good, and the site was very intuitive. The resultant product was high-quality and did not disappoint. It also has a cool tool to be able to experiment with pricing. And it is nice for the customer to have the freedom to select between less costly paper-bound to higher cost hardcover or paper wrap.

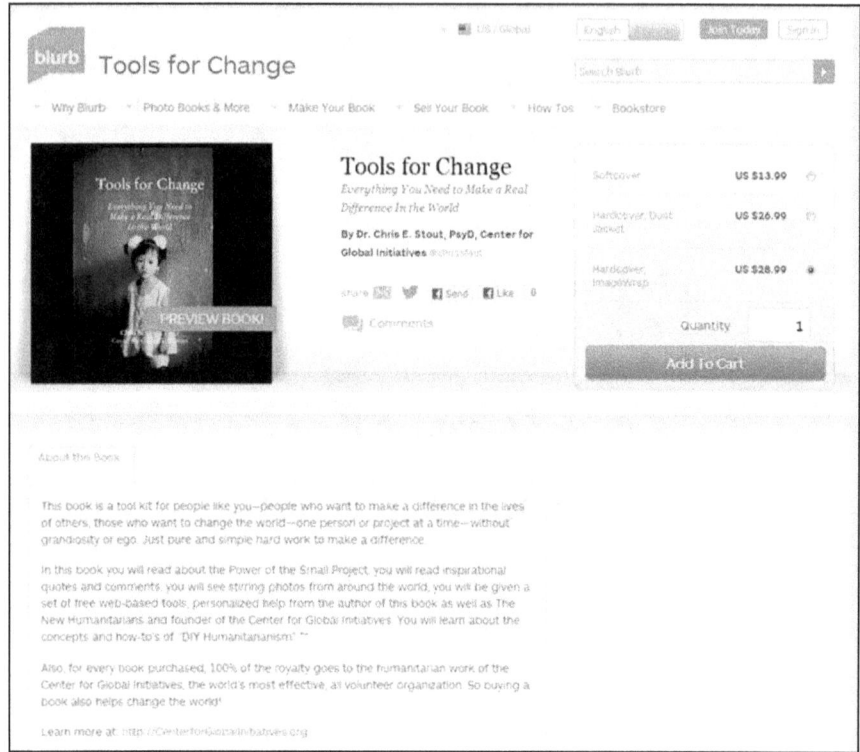

LuLu

Lulu is very similar to Blurb, and a primary peer/competitor. I've not used them, but they are very well respected and worth a look-see.

Chris E. Stout

Chapter 17

Amazon's CreateSpace & Kindle

By Chris E Stout

This book is a CreateSpace production and is available on Kindle. It is my third with them. Needless to say, I have a bias to Amazon as they are king of the jungle. Their printing costs are the lowest, and there are no initial set-up fees. They offer a non-exclusive agreement that keeps your future publishing and distribution options open as well. Nice.

As noted earlier, you gain a larger royalty, receive

reduced printing costs and gain access to an expanded distribution channel. If you need some self-publishing services (editing, formatting, book design, cover design, marketing and publicity) CreateSpace offers them for additional fees or you can do them yourself and then use CreateSpace to publish and distribute your book.

Amazon basically helps you potentially reach more than a billion readers worldwide. Your work will be accessible via the Kindle itself, but also via a Kindle app for nearly every major web browser, smartphone platform and for both Windows and Mac-based computers.

Chapter 19

How To Publish
Your Book on Amazon

By Chris E. Stout

I have found Kindle/CreateSpace to be very user friendly. The following is a walk through to help you get started should you consider using them for your self-published book.

1. Sign Up To Publish

At the bottom of Amazon's home page is a link to "independently publish with us." Click the link. You are ready to publish to Kindle.

2. Create Kindle Publishing Account

Click "Get Started" to begin.

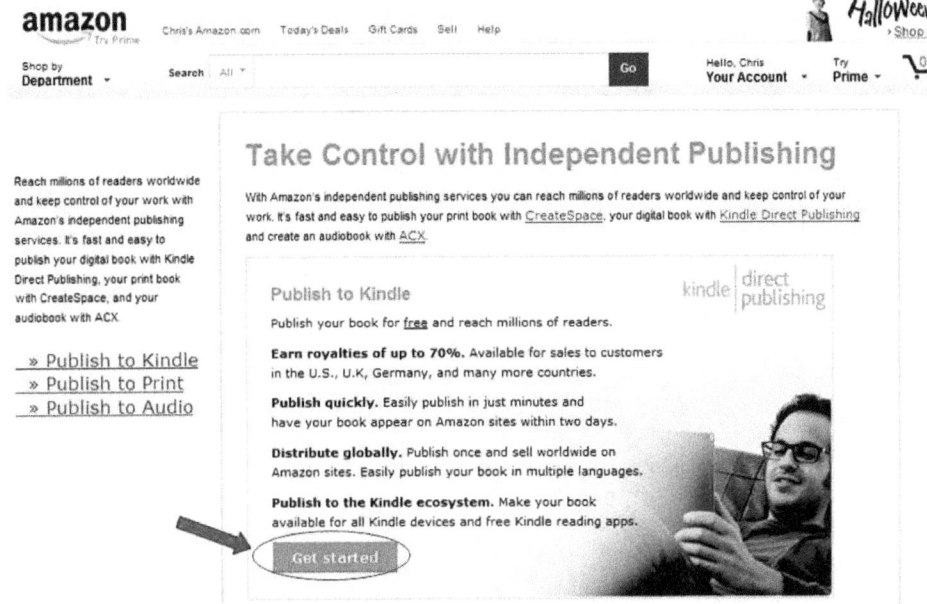

You will need to use your existing Amazon account or create one. Note: You may be required to provide additional information, including your banking information, as Amazon will wire your royalties to your account on a monthly basis for balances over $10.00.

3. Add Title

With an account created, Amazon takes you to your "Kindle Dashboard." This is where you will add your works and access reports on book sales.

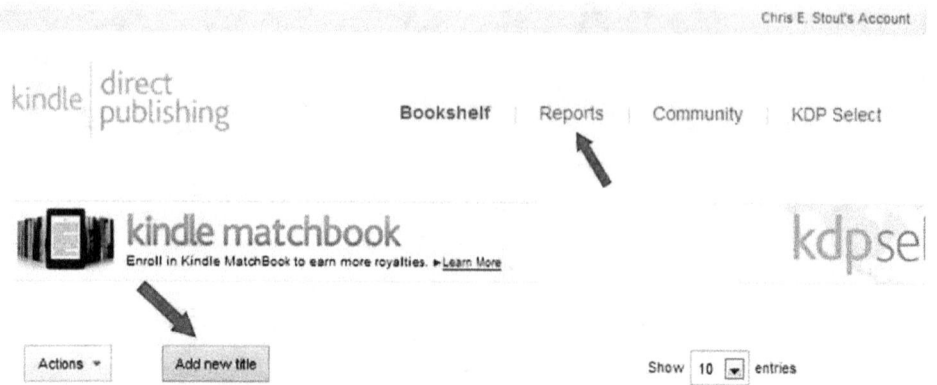

If your work is ready to be published, click on "Add New Title."

4. Enter Your Book Details

Here you provide Amazon with details on your book, including title, authorship, book type, pricing and more. You do not need to have an ISBN code when using Amazon as they'll assign one for you, for free.

1. Enter Your Book Details

Book name

New Title 1

Please enter the exact title only. Books submitted with extra words in this field will not be published. (Why?)

☐ This book is part of a series (What's this?)

Edition number (optional) (What's this?)

Publisher (optional) (What's this?)

Description (What's this?)

4000 characters left

Book contributors: (What's this?)

Add contributors

Language (What's this?)   Publication date (optional)

English

ISBN (optional) (What's this?)

5. Book Category

Amazon encourages you to add up to two "categories" for your book. This can include everything from "Antiques & Collectibles" to "Dystopian Fiction."

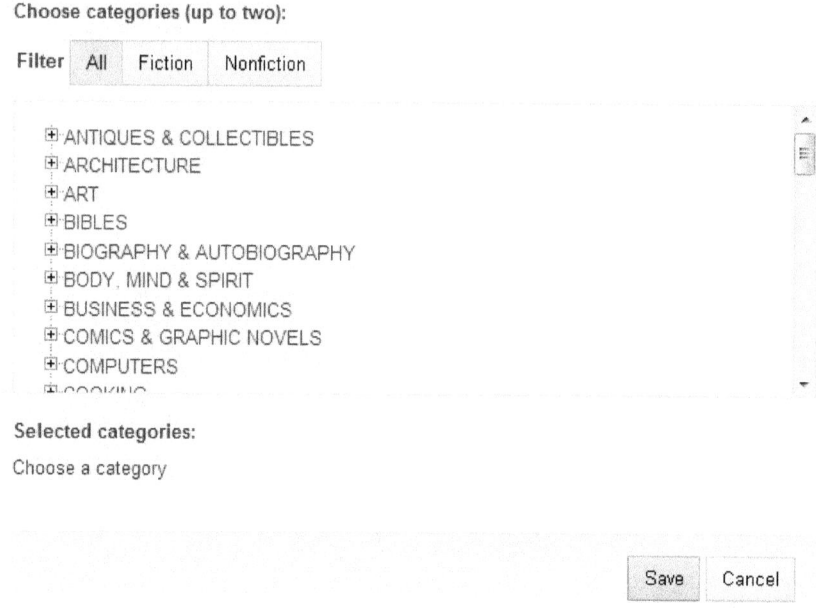

Recommendation: Chances are your book crosses more than two categories. Search Amazon for the book(s) that you think is most like yours. In the details page, Amazon includes the categories selected for that book. Use those.

3. Target Your Book to Customers

Categories (What's this?)

Add Categories

Search keywords (up to 7, optional) (What's this?)

7 keywords left

You can also add up to seven keywords, so think of the words your audience would use to find your work in a browser search.

6. Give Your Book A Cover

Even an eBook should have a cover, although it is not required. Amazon provides guidelines for uploading cover images and also includes a rather limited tool to create your own cover. I have monkeyed with two of my books' covers, but fell in love with Cover Lover Software. It is an independent ebook publishing tool that helps authors create an amazing cover for their book. I used it for the cover of this book.

Some FAQs about the software from their site:

Can I add my own images in Cover Lover?

Yes! In the "Media" window click the "Add" button, choose your file, and give it a name, click Save. Once your image is added you will see it in the Media window. Each image added will show as the last image in the window so you might have to scroll down to locate it. Click and drag the image to the template. You can resize the image by grabbing the handles. The templates are high resolution with a width of 1500px and a height of 2400px, images needs to be high resolution as well.

How do I save my cover?

Click the Save button and your cover will be saved as a cls file. When you are ready to work on the cover again locate the saved cls file by clicking "Load A Saved Template" on the welcome screen.

Click the Export button and your cover will be saved as a JPG file directly.

See for yourself: http://coverloverapp.com

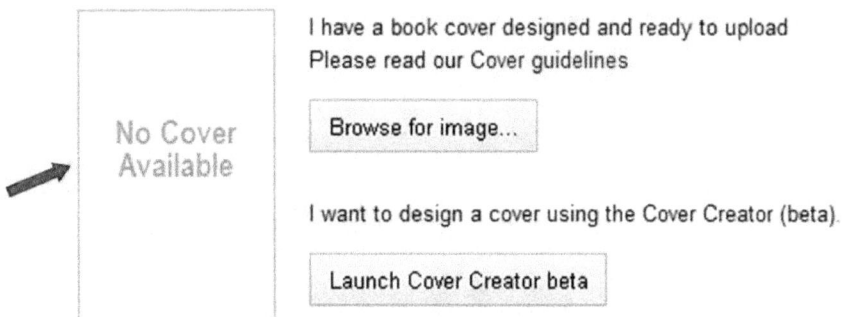

7. Time To Upload Your Book

Now comes the fun-scary part: uploading your book!

5. Upload Your Book File

Select a digital rights management (DRM) option: (What's this?)

○ Enable digital rights management

⦿ Do not enable digital rights management

Book content file:

[Browse]

Learn KDP content guidelines
Help with formatting
Create a comic book for Kindle

You'll be asked you want to enable digital rights management (DRM) or not. I recommend doing so as it makes it harder for others to share your work and potentially harder for it to be copied and sold without payment. Then just upload your manuscript from your computer.

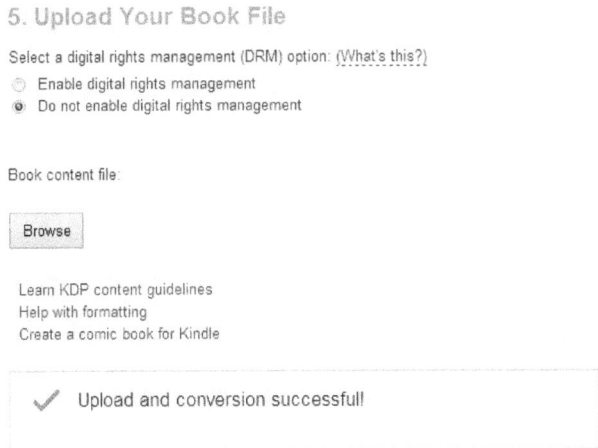

Amazon accepts the following formats

- Word (DOC and DOCX)
- HTML
- ePub
- Text
- PDF

8. Formatting and Previewing

I first consider the size of my book and then download the template they provide and work within that template. I have done it other ways in the past and regretted it. You should always preview your work even after successfully uploading it. I pay the minimal fee for a hardcopy proof as it never fails that I find a mistake or ugly formatting in the hardcopy proof that I missed digitally.

My first and second books had a number of tables and the like and it was a pain to get right. So you may need to use a special program for that and then save the document in PDF format. Amazon's upload service should retain the proper formatting.

After uploading your work, use the "Online Previewer" link to see how your book will look on different devices. Then, from the drop down list, Amazon lets you see what your book will look like on select Kindle devices, iPhone and iPad. If you wish to see how it will look on other devices, or in a browser, you will need to download the "previewer" tool.

9. Set Your Price

Amazon lets you set nearly any price you wish for your book. However, there are two different royalty options: 35% or 70%. Obviously, you want the 70% royalty.

8. Choose Your Royalty

Please select a royalty option for your book. (What's this?)

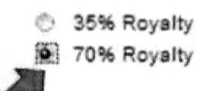

○ 35% Royalty
◉ 70% Royalty

	List Price	Royalty Rate	Delivery Costs	Estimated Royalty
Amazon.com	$ 3.99 USD Price must be between $2.99 and $9.99	35% (Why?)	n/a	$1.40
		70%	$0.25	$2.62
Amazon.in (What's this?)	☑ Set IN price automatically based on US price Rs245 ⚠ Your book must be enrolled in KDP Select in order to be eligible for 70% royalty for sales in India. Enroll now	35%	n/a	Rs86
Amazon.co.uk	☐ Set UK price automatically based on US price £ 2.50 GBP Price must be between £1.49 and £7.81.	70%	£0.17	£1.63
Amazon.de	☐ Set DE price automatically based on US price € 2.90 EUR Price must be between €2.60 and €9.70.	70%	€0.20	€1.89

Having said that, do consider that:

- If you price your book below $2.99, Amazon will only offer the 35% royalty option.

- In some smaller markets, Amazon only offers the 35% royalty. (The 70% option is available in the U.S., Canada, UK and most larger markets.)

- When you choose the 70% royalty option, Amazon also deducts a small "delivery fee" for each book sold. This is their additional fee for wirelessly distributing your work, and is based on the file size of your work. In the U.S., this fee is presently set at 15 cents per megabyte. (A Word document of approximately 100,000 words and with minimal graphics is typically no more than 1 MB.)

- There is no delivery charge with the 35% royalty option.

Doing the math, if you set a $2.99 price for your book, and choose the 70% royalty option, your royalty for each book sold is likely to be:

$2.99 x .70 = $2.09 before delivery fee

$2.09 - .15 (delivery fee) = $1.94.

You earn $1.94 for each book sold. You also have the

ability to designate your book for sale in only certain countries, or worldwide.

10. Finished!

It usually takes Amazon about 24-48 hours before your book is actually available for sale. You may also want to consider their "KDP Select" program. With KDP Select, if you agree to publish your work on Kindle—exclusively—for 90 (or so) days and allow Amazon customers to borrow it for free, Amazon will pay you a small fee each time the book is borrowed. Typically, this fee is close to the royalty you would have received had the book actually been purchased. I have done this as I didn't see a down side to experimenting and I was not publishing on iTunes or the like.

Introducing KDP Select

Introducing KDP Select – a new option to make money and promote your book. When you make your book exclusive to Kindle for at least 90 days, it will be part of the Kindle Owner's Lending Library for the same period and you will earn your share of a monthly fund when readers borrow your books from the library. You can also promote your book as free for up to 5 days during these 90 days. While in KDP Select you will also be eligible to earn 70% royalty for sales to customers in India. Learn more

☐ **Enroll this book in KDP Select**
By checking the box, you are enrolling in KDP Select. Books enrolled in KDP Select must not be available in digital format on any other platform during their enrollment. If your book is found to be available elsewhere in digital format, it may not be eligible to remain in the program. See the KDP Select Terms and Conditions for more details.

Amazon obviously wants everyone to have their work available exclusively through Amazon.

Chapter 19

How to Create Your First Kindle Book This Weekend

By Ryan Deiss

Writing a book doesn't have to be painful. In fact, it can actually be a lot of fun if you follow this 7-step process, and once your research is done (Steps 1 – 5), the actually "writing" can be completed in just 1 hour (or a few if you take your time)…

…so let's dive in and get started!

NOTE: The process below works best for non-fiction books, but you can use the index card strategy to lay out plots and characters for fiction books as well.

Step #1 – Buy and read at least 3 top books on your subject, and read all the blog posts for the last 60 days for the top 6 blogs in your market.

Step #2 – Interview at least 6 experts in the field to get an idea of the different positions and opinions on key issues.

Step #3 – Compile your notes from the interviews as well as the primary points you learned from reading the books into one file folder.

Step #4 – Take 12 index and write a question on each card.

Step #5 – Get 120 more index cards (12 for each remaining chapter) and write sub-chapter titles on one side and three words on the other side to remind you what you want to say in this section.

Step #6 – Write 250 – 700 words for each sub-chapter or record yourself talking about that sub-chapter for 3 - 5 minutes.

SECTION IV

Marketing

Chapter 20

Help Readers Discover Your Books on Amazon

By CreateSpaceResources

If you want to sell more books worldwide, readers must first be able to find them. With millions of books published each year, how can you increase your title's chances of success?

The following simple steps can improve your title's discoverability on Amazon.co.uk, Amazon.de, Amazon.fr,

Amazon.it, and Amazon.es, all available by enrolling your titles in free Amazon Europe distribution via your CreateSpace member dashboard. These tips are applicable not only to Amazon's European channels, but also to Amazon.com, so read on to discover ways you can help drive more traffic to your books both in the U.S. and internationally.

The Discoverability Trifecta

To help improve the discoverability of your books, start by focusing on three main areas:

1. Getting the basics right with the relevancy and quality of the data you provide.

2. Ensuring your Amazon Author Pages are claimed and used on Amazon.com and each of its European websites.

3. Using social networking and Amazon Associates programs on Amazon.com and each of its European channels to help drive traffic.

These three things will help you get the most out of your book's listings on Amazon.com and Amazon's European websites.

Get the Basics Right

Ensuring that all the relevant background data - or metadata - is complete and accurate when you submit your title is a great way to give your book the best start at attracting an audience. Concentrate on the following areas:

- **Short Description** - Providing a complete and relevant product description will give customers visibility and clarity about what a book is about. When writing the description, imagine you're the customer: what information is most important and meaningful and will help you make that buying decision? Keep things simple, and keep them relevant.

- **BIC and BISAC Subject Codes** - Knowing the correct BIC and BISAC codes for your titles will help the Amazon team categorize them correctly onsite and will help customers find your titles when they're browsing. Don't just choose the high level code; dig a little deeper and make that classification as relevant as possible. For example, a book classified as "Fiction / Romance / Historical" would more easily be found by an interested reader in that genre than a book simply listed as "Fiction."

- **Keywords** - Accurate keywords can make it easier for your customers to find your book. These are a great opportunity for you to associate the right words or search terms with your book, even if they're not included in the title or the subject codes. Keywords should be authentic, applicable, and relevant to maximize their utility. You can add 5, but you might not need that many; don't be tempted to use them all just because you can, because relevancy is the most important factor here. You can do this when you add additional information in the "Distribute" section when you're setting up a title. There is no need to repeat existing information like title, author name, or ISBN in your keywords.

Amazon Author Pages

Amazon Author Pages are a great way to keep your readers up to date about you and your work. You can create your Author Pages on Amazon.com and many of its European websites though Amazon Author Central. You must create a separate Author Page on each of the websites you want to appear. You can sign up for your Amazon Author Pages at each of the following sites:

- Amazon.com
- Amazon.co.uk
- Amazon.de
- Amazon.fr

On your Author Pages, provide a concise and meaningful author biography to help your readers get to know you. You can also upload a photograph and videos, add your Twitter handle, and even highlight events you may be attending. Author Pages also bring together all of your work as an author in one place, which helps customers discover more of your books. Use Amazon Author Pages to make a direct connection with your audience.

Associate Pages and Social Networking

As an independent author, it's up to you to be your own biggest advocate. You can harness the power of social networking tools like Facebook and Twitter to reach international audiences and drive traffic to your Amazon detail pages or Author Pages on Amazon.com and each European channel.

As well as driving sales for your books, you can also take advantage of Amazon Associates programs. The programs enable you to easily create links from your website or social networking pages to an Amazon product page; you earn advertising fees based on the revenue generated as a result of these links. Since Amazon has Associates programs in each of its European channels, you can drive your book marketing traffic to these stores based on the specific audience you're targeting. To find out more, visit Amazon Associates on Amazon.com, Amazon.co.uk, Amazon.de, Amazon.fr, Amazon.it, and Amazon.es.

Taking advantage of each of the three areas described above will give your book a better chance of being noticed and purchased by readers. By enabling and using the tools available to you on Amazon.com and each of its European websites, you'll be better positioned to reach your goals and achieve international indie success.

Chapter 21

How to Sell 100 Kindle Books a Day

By Ryan Deiss

Market Selection

Picking the right market, especially in Kindle, is half the game.

There's a balance that you have to strike between finding a niche that you can dominate, and selling enough books in that niche each month that it matters.

For example, I'm pretty sure that I can dominate the ant farming niche in Kindle, but I doubt very many ant farming books get sold every day… so what's the point?

The point I'm trying to make is, it's really easy in Kindle to be the "King of the Hill"… you just want to make sure your "hill" is more like a mountain than a mole hill.

The best way to assess market size is by looking at "Amazon's Sellers Rank" figures. (This figure can be found under every book.

There's a Kindle Sales Rank Calculator over at:

http://www.kdpcalculator.com

…that will tell you, with pretty decent accuracy, how many books are being sold in Amazon for any title at any given time, but here are some general "rules of thumb" so you can get a sense of how "Sellers Rank" can help you determine sales volumes.

Based on our research, books with a Sellers Rank of 1000 to 3000 average 20 – 30 sales per day.

Books in the 10,000 Sales Rank range tend to sell 3 - 6 copies per day, and books in the 30,000 range only sell 2 – 3 copies per day.

Again, for more accurate estimates you can use KDPCalculator.com ...

...just remember that any number is an estimate, at best, because Amazon keeps their data proprietary.

Either way, if the top books in your category all have a Sellers Rank above 30,000, that's probably a market that will be fairly easy to own.

The FREE to Paid Model

There are two schools of thought when it comes to Kindle book promotion strategies.

Some publishers believe that you should never give away your book for free.

They feel that it diminishes the value of the book, and the fact that you have to sometimes spend money to give away a book seems counterintuitive to them.

I will admit, a good argument can be made for their way of thinking…if (and only if) you have a substantial promotional budget at your disposal or a big, fat email subscriber list.

Anyone who wants to spend enough money can advertise and promote their book the top of any Kindle category.

That's an absolute fact.

But I'm operating under the assumption that you are NOT sitting on thousands of dollars that you can spend on promotions, or a multi-thousand person email subscriber list.

If that's the case, then I invite you to read on and see how we drive books to the top of their categories WITHOUT spending a fortune on advertising.

I call it, the "Free To Paid Method"…

5 Magic Days

Amazon has a program called the KDP Select program that I found to be a very useful tool in the promotion of my Kindle books. You can choose to enroll your book in KDP Select as the very first step in the upload process…

But this program is not without its "gotchas"…

#1. Amazon requires 90 days of exclusivity for any ebook you enroll into KDP Select. In other words, you can't sell or give away your book on any other site (including your own) for a full 3 months.

That means you have to wait to publish your book on other channels such as Apple, Barnes and Noble, Android and Sony. This is definitely a bummer, but as you're about to see it's a sacrifice worth making.

#2. Amazon Prime members are allowed to borrow your book without purchasing it. This sounds bad, at first, but fortunately they do pay you for these free "Borrows".

Currently this fee is ranging between $1.40 and $1.70 per book borrowed, which is certainly better than a sharp stick in the eye.

For example, over the past few weeks our "How To Use Pinterest" ebook has sold around 400 copies, making me around $2 per copy.

In addition, that same book is been borrowed about 190 times, making me an additional $300 ($1.70 per copy) which is money I wouldn't have made if I were not enrolled in the KDP program.

In addition to the extra money, Amazon also allows KDP participants to give away their book for free for 5 days every 90 days as a promotion.

Here's the big zinger. Amazon counts those books that are downloaded for free as sales, and allows reviewers from those sales to be listed as verified purchasers in the reviews.

This is huge.

In other words, you can let people download your book for free and then give a review of your book as if they paid money for it.

These reviews go a long way with Amazon buyers.

The Goal

There are really two goals that you should keep in mind if you decide to make a free promotional run on your book.

#1 Downloads – The sheer number of downloads a book gets seems to make a big difference in how well it sells after the free download period.

Based on our research, you will sell between 3% and 5% as many books in the 1st month after a free promotion as you gave away, and that number tends to hold for 3–4 months.

In other words, a book that you give away 10,000 copies should sell between 300 and 500 copies the next month.

And the really good news is that by the time the book sales begin to slow, you'll have another 5 day giveaway period to re-promote it…

…and the cycle continues.

#2 Reviews - Reviews sell books. I learned this lesson the hard way on my 3rd attempt at Kindle publishing.

It was a tongue-in-cheek political comedy about the current presidential candidate, and to be fair, the writer is also producing a "50 Shades of Obama" book so we can be an equal-opportunity offender. :)

But all politics aside, here's what I learned from this book launch:

Polarizing subjects like politics and religion make for poorly reviewed books, no matter how good the book is.

In this case, this particular book received either 5-star or 1-star reviews. There was no in between.

Why?

Again, it had nothing to do with the quality of the book. If the reader was a Democrat, they thought it was great. If they were a Republican, they thought it was terrible.

The real net result was that the book was not a very good seller, even though I employed the same promotional strategies that we used with all our other books.

At the end of the day, the bad reviews killed the book and it never gained the momentum it needed to get off the ground.

(But for what it's worth, even as a dud this book still sells a few hundred copies a month after 6898 free downloads. That's $200 - $300 NET MONEY for a relative "flop". Not too shabby...)

On the other hand, with the "How To Use Pinterest" book we received over 60 four-star and five-star reviews in just a few days, effectively locking the book's position as the number one book on Pinterest for all of Kindle.

7 Proven Promotional Ideas

Now let's talk about how you actually promote your book both during the free promotional time and after the book is in paid status.

Remember, the number one objective is to give away a lot of books and there's no better place to do that and on freebie sites.

1. Freebie Sites

One of the easiest ways to "juice" your Kindle downloads is to offer your book for free on one of the many "freebie" sites on the web.

Here's a list of a few freebie sites that I usually contact when we want to give away one of our books:

http://www.TotallyFreeStuff.com
http://www.icravefreebies.com
http://www.FreeStuffUnlimited.com

NOTE: You can Google "free stuff" and "freebies" for even more sites and forums just like the ones above.

The good news is the people on these sites do download a lot of books. The bad news is they don't really read them, so reviews will be low and future conversions will be even lower.

For this exercise it really doesn't matter. Right now, all you want is downloads so you can push your book higher and higher in its category. Once it's at the top, the "real" readers will start buying...

2. Free Kindle Sites

The very best place to promote your book during the free promotional period are freebie sites designed specifically for free Kindle books.

Here's a list of some of the ones that you should approach:

http://www.PixelofInk.com

http://www.BookReaderNewsToday.com

https://www.facebook.com/pages/Free-Kindle-Books/489529967728474

But before you approach these "Free Kindle" websites, there's something you need to keep in mind...

Most of these sites don't accept advertising and will only promote your book if they like it or you. I would not approach the sites until your book already has at least 5 positive reviews. And above all else, remember that the site owners are doing you a favor...so be nice.

3. Niche Forums

If your book is on a niche topic (or what I call a passion a topic) niche forums are a great way to give away your book.

However, you do need to plan in advance, as most of these forums will not simply let you register and post a message about your book the same day.

So for example, if you're planning to write a book about fishing, you might want to go make yourself familiar with all the top fishing forums and began chatting it up with other fishermen 30 – 60 days BEFORE your book goes live.

That way when, you put out your book for free, it will be from an active member doing a nice thing, versus a spammer crashing their fishing community.

4. Facebook Fan Pages and Groups

Facebook is a powerfully viral tool for the Kindle publisher.

There are literally hundreds of pages dedicated to freebies, free Kindle books, and niche passion topics.

Participating these groups is easy. Simply search your topic as if you are looking for an old friend on Facebook.

To find the most powerful pages you may consider doing a Google search like the one below. (Search string: "keyword" facebook.com)

Think some of them might be interested in downloading your free Kindle book? You bet they would!

And best of all, once you're a "fan" of the page (or a member of the group), you can write posts on the page for all the members to see.

Just remember, be cool and DO NOT SPAM!!!

Contribute to the community and to the conversation, and no one will complain when you casually comment that you're giving your book away free for 5 days on Amazon.com.

5. Remnant Ads

If you have a few dollars to spend, remnant ads are a great choice.

"Remnant ads" are ads that have gone unsold, so you're able to lock them down for dirt-cheap prices.

These types of ads are typically not very effective at selling products, but when you're giving away a Kindle book for free they can be VERY powerful.

And again, they're wicked cheap…

I use a site called Sitescout.com that allows me to buy banner ads at around $.10 - $.20 per 1000 impressions…

…that's pretty dang cheap.

I usually end up spending around $0.20 to send clicks to my Amazon book during my free promotional period.

Unfortunately, Amazon doesn't give me analytics or statistics that tells me which of these viewers actually downloaded the book, but I assume because the book is free it's a fairly high percentage.

6. Press Releases

Getting your book into the press will help you in two different ways.

First, it will get the word out about giving away your book for free.

Most of our press releases will drive between 300-1000 clicks back to our Amazon sales pages.

The service that I like using the most is the press release syndication from Webwire. com…

We use several others services that are more expensive, but they seem to do a pretty good job.

The second big benefit from using press releases is SEO.

Have you noticed that no matter what subject you search on Google, there's typically an Amazon listing in the top 5?

This is a big part of our strategy in the long term, but I don't have time to cover it here. Just know that the extra inbound links from these press releases to your Amazon page go a long way to ensuring that YOUR Amazon page appears in the top of Google…and not your competition.

7. Private Masterminds

Probably the most powerful tool in our arsenal is having friends who are also Amazon publishers.

Over the last year or so, a number of private masterminds have formed of writers and publishers who have agreed to download and review each others' books during their 5-day promotional periods.

This absolutely ensures the success of most books.

And the bigger the network, the higher your chances of success.

This is the main reason we created our "Number One Book System" and the "Number One Book Club" over at:

http://www.numberonebooksystem.com

I want to build the largest writer and publisher mastermind in the world.

You'll learn a lot more about this club (and the training that accompanies it) in the coming days, but if for some reason you don't participate in the Number One Book Club, you should start building your own private networks now.

After Free Promotions

Once your book switches to paid, things change quite a lot.

You should be earning roughly $2.06 per $2.99 book that you sell, which means just a dozen or so sales a day could very well cover your car payment. Not bad, eh?

Here are a couple of ways that we promote books after they go to the paid category.

1. Google PPC

Yep, good old Google AdWords: http://adwords.google.com

While Google will not allow you to run ads directly to your Amazon page, they will allow you to run ads to your own web page where you can then direct folks over to Amazon.

Currently, I'm experimenting with mini-video sales letters that send people over to purchase my Amazon books. The sales letters only last 3 to 5 minutes and can be created with PowerPoint in 30 minutes or less.

I typically only use Google ads to prime the pump when my sales rankings are slipping in Amazon as the ads typically do not ROI.

In other words, I may be spending $3 to make $2, but I only have to do it for a few days until my book goes back to the top of its category an Amazon marketing takes over.

2. Facebook Ads

Similar to Google Adwords, Facebook ads are another effective way to drive people to buy your book.

While Facebook ads are typically less expensive per click than Google, they usually don't convert as well so the ROI winds up working out more or less the same.

There are a number of tricks that you can use to increase your conversion from any PPC Amazon campaign.

One of the bigger ones is making sure that your buyer realizes when they click the buy button are going to Amazon. That way they know they're going to a retailer they trust, and there are no up-sells or shenanigans.

3. YouTube

The little mini video sales letters I talked about above are working quite well in some niche topics in YouTube.

And it's fairly easy to get a YouTube video to rank high in Google (especially if you utilize the Press Release method I talked about earlier), so if you play your cards right you could end up having both a YouTube video and your Amazon page in the top of Google for your primary keywords.

Using YouTube to sell Kindle books that are below $5 is a very effective strategy and one that we will be using in volume in the future. But fair warning: It doesn't work nearly as well if you price your book above $10.

4. SEO

Lastly, we usually make a $20 - $50 investment in the SEO of our Amazon books every 90 days or so.

While SEO has become increasingly difficult for websites, it's still quite easy to use basic SEO tactics to rank Amazon pages in Google because Amazon.com is such a high-authority website.

SIDE NOTE: I don't want to dive into SEO too much because it's a topic that deserves its own book series. Just know that the higher the authority

of a given site, the easier it is to get individual pages on that site to rank high in Google.

Here's an example of fellow writer's Kindle book that ranks on Google for very competitive category based on his spending just a few dollars in basic search engine marketing every few months.

Key Takeaways

Here the big takeaways that you should remember from this report.

Number 1. Nothing is better than having a community of friends to help you promote your books. With enough people supporting you, you can absolutely rule your category.

SHAMELESS PLUG: I obviously can't recommend my own community enough. Get the details by going to: http://www.numberonebooksystem.com

Number 2. If you have to spend a few bucks to promote your book you'll only have to do it for a short period time to prime the pump.

Remember, Amazon is the greatest bookseller in the history of mankind. Get your book to the top of listings and Amazon will sell for you.

Number 3. Getting your book in the hands of thousands of people for free is far easier than you think, and getting those people to give you reviews will be faster than if you sold your book one at a time.

Number 4. Kindle is here to stay. I'm sure if you've read this far, you have to agree that Kindle is ruling (and will continue to rule) the book and ebook markets for some time to come.

Number 5. You have a level playing field, at least for a while, to compete with the big boys like Simon & Schuster and Random House.

If you miss this, you'll regret it for very long time. Don't let that happen!

Publish your Kindle book today, and claim your slice of the book market while you still can. Thanks a lot for taking the time to read this report and I hope to have you as a fellow publisher in the Number One Book Club.

Chris E. Stout

Chapter 22

Marketing Ideas and Approaches

By Chris E. Stout

I have experimented with various approaches with different books in terms of promotion. I was very excited back in the 1990's when Wiley got one of my books featured in the Behavioral Sciences Book Club. I had no idea that it was to be listed, and as a member, I was thrilled with the surprise to see it.

That was then, this is now...

Getting "Names" as Endorsements

I have found this is really pretty easy. The key is to simply ask. Now, the "ask" is just about it if it is with someone who already knows you or your work. It is helpful for that person if you can send them a pre-print or galley proof of the book so they can cogently speak in support of it. Ideally, working with your publisher, see if the endorsements can appear on the back cover. You can then use them on websites and other promotional materials once the book is getting ready to be launched or after it is published.

If you do not know the person, see if you can find someone who knows both that person and you. Then he or she can serve as a conduit and hopefully increase the likelihood for you to get the endorsement you're seeking.

It is not unusual for the person endorsing your book to ask you to ghostwrite the endorsement or provide some draft that he or she can edit to their voice and make their own. It is helpful for them and generally it helps you feel comfortable that it will be done on time and hit the high notes as you see them.

You may also want to get notable and relevant professional colleague to write your Foreword or Afterword. The process is the same, but it is an obligation for the person to have to write more. Please appreciate that this is a VERY nice favor to you and your book, and be sure to convey your thanks and appreciation many, many times. Keep the Karma going when someone in the future asks you to do such for their book.

Mehmet Oz (yes, TV's "*Dr. Oz*")is a friend and wrote the Foreword to my three volume Praeger published *The New Humanitarians.* It was very kind of him and I let him know it.

Pinterest

I've just recently joined Pinterest and I have created a "Library" Board and posted my books therein. See:

http://www.pinterest.com/drchrisstout/library

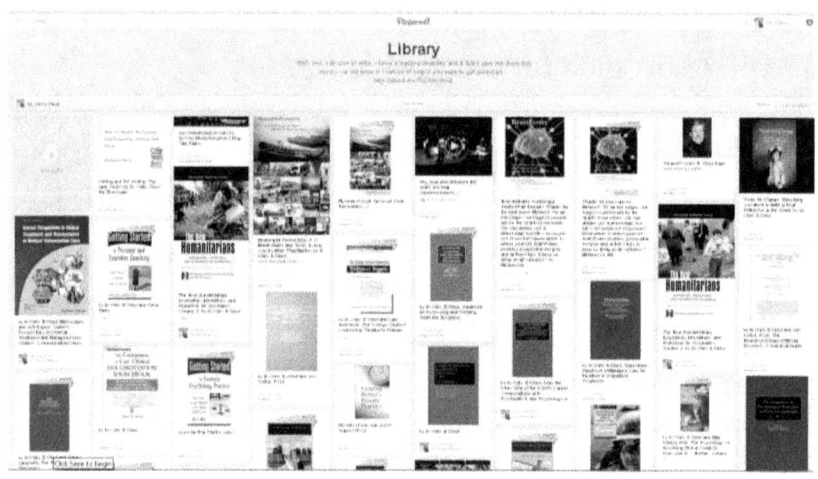

I have also created a board on Presentations that allows for not only images, but also YouTube videos and SlideShare presentations. See:

http://www.pinterest.com/drchrisstout/presentations

I'm not sure what impact these have, but I believe that the more places people can find you or stumble upon you, the better.

Amazon Best Sellers Rank

No one was more surprised than me to see some of my books rank highly on Amazon. While it isn't the *New York Times*, it is nevertheless a very respectable accomplishment for a book, and as so, should be made known.

It's not like Amazon sends you an email saying "Congratulations," so you need to go looking for it yourself. Circled below is the #11 ranking of my Wiley book, *Getting Started in Private Practice*. It is on the page where the book is, down in the Product Details section. Note the ranking is based in its category, so it is not up against Steven King (thankfully).

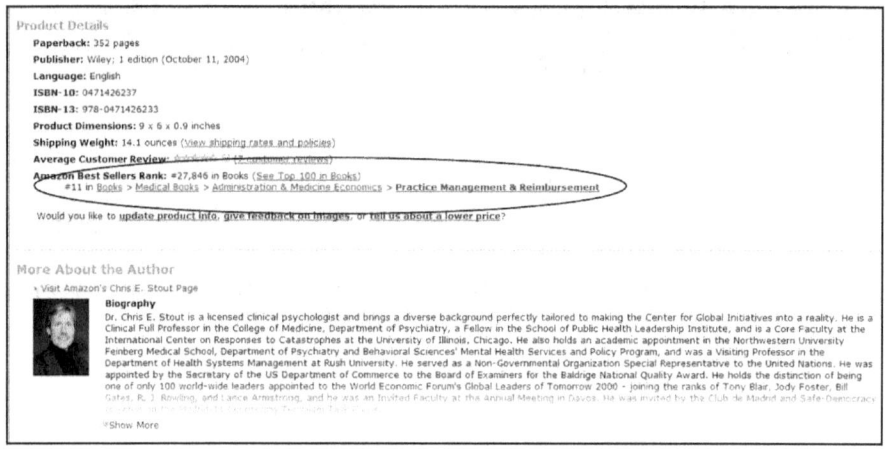

I should also note that this screen shot was made at least eight years after its publication, so that's somewhat cool. You just never know when your book will rank well (or at least I do not), so you may want to periodically check in.

Having said that, about three weeks following my publishing (again with Wiley), *Getting Better in Private Practice*, it was ranked at number five(!). A you can see below, here I was looking for my book in its category.

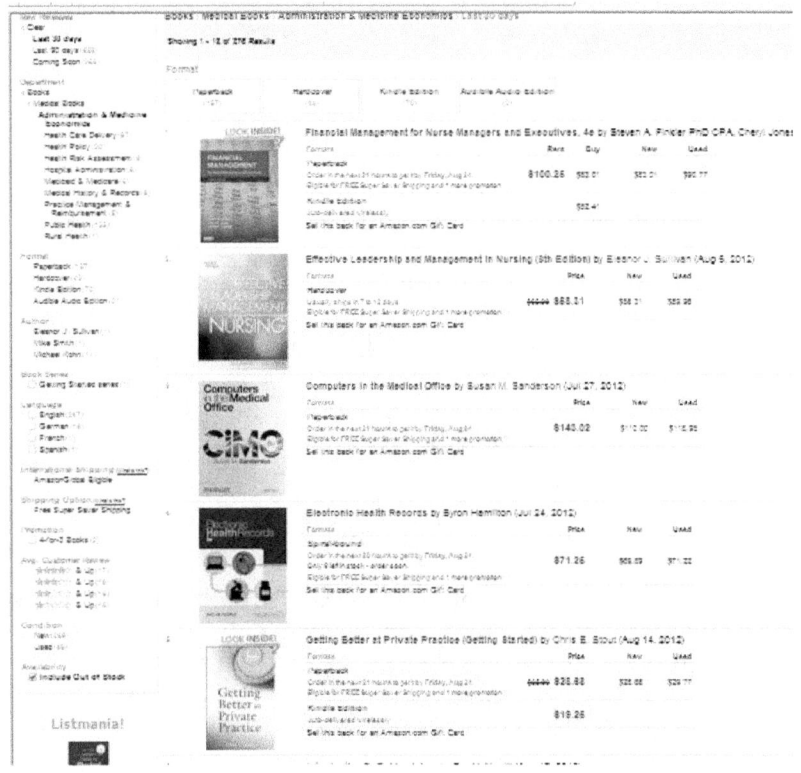

I was interviewed about this book and I used this screen shot when I sent in my media materials. The interviewer mentioned it on-air, which was great, and it is a great tool to support your claim of ranking status.

Oprah On Line 1

As you now likely realize, just because your book is published, your work is not done. Now you need to get the word out. Here are eight tips to get started:

1. Participate in online forums about your book's subject.

2. Ask colleagues, friends and book bloggers if they would review your book. Don't forget to offer them a free copy of your book. Digital is fine.

3. Create a mailing list composed of people who have shown interest in your work. Keep them informed about anything new that you've written.

4. Go to Amazon Central to create an author profile so readers can learn more about you. Mine is at: http://www.amazon.com/Chris-E.-Stout/e/B003MROVZ8 and it looks like this:

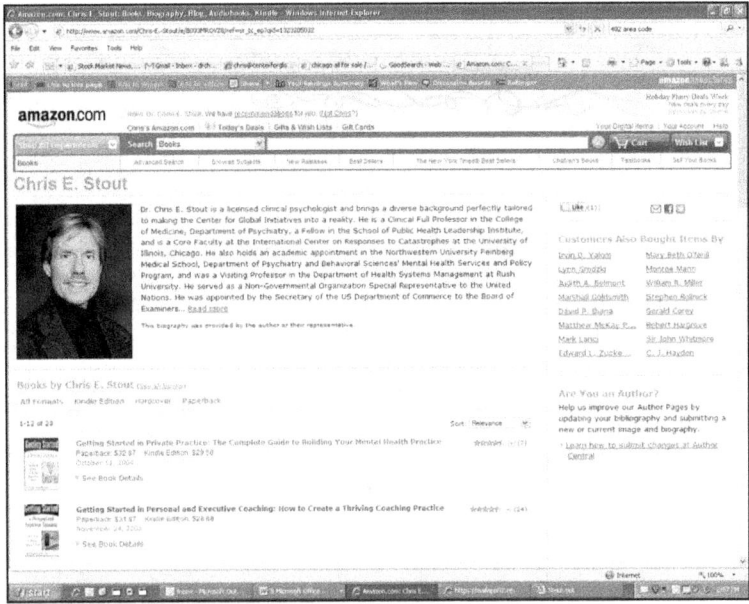

5. Make a news- or press-release and email it to your local media (local TV news, local cable, radio).

6. Contact local libraries and do a talk on your book and or its topical area. I have found that doing so generally comes with a modest, but nice stipend, and it is very fun to do.

7. Also consider a local coffee place, a bookstore, etc. I did a talk at Barnes and Noble and it was also fun. Don't expect a check, but do hope to sell and sign your books.

8. If you are a psychologist, you may want to join the American Psychological Association's media referral

services. Be ready to define your specific expertise. Then, be prompt in returning journalists' phone calls and helping them develop their stories. If you are in a different profession see what you guild may have along these lines.

Website Promotion

My buddy Holly Hunt, PhD, created a website (http://www.essentialsofprivatepractice.com)dedicated to promote her book of the same name (*Essentials of Private Practice*) and her related consulting services. It's great and today needs to be a standard.

I have a non-profit organization
(http://centerforglobalinitiatives.org/), and on its website I have a
description of my book-set, *The New Humanitarians.* So
while it is not a standalone site, it makes sense to be where
it is.

I am also starting to get Linkedin emails from others to promote their books. I think that is clever. Here is a sample from a friend and colleague:

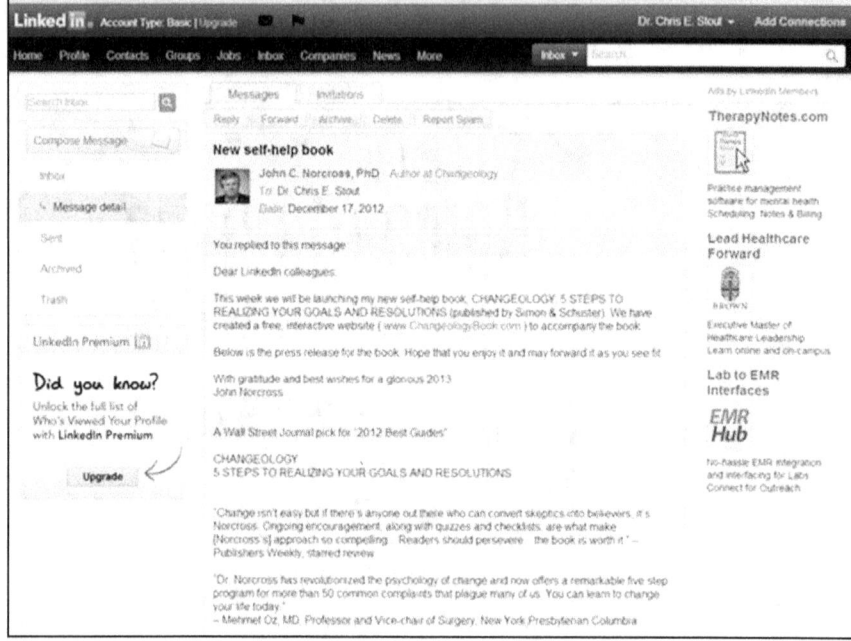

Chapter 23

Buying Your Way onto

Bestseller Lists

By Steve O'Keefe

In a recent issue of The Wall Street Journal, long-time publishing correspondent Jeffrey A. Trachtenberg outed book PR firm ResultSource for engineering appearances on bestseller lists for clients' books.

The method the ResultSource was using is tried-and-true in the world of business books: They bought their way onto these lists.

In a dramatic example of PR bravado, UCLA Health System paid ResultSource to mail a copy of a book about them to every hospital CEO in the USA. Instead of having approximately 13,000 books printed then shipped via a fulfillment service, UCLA Health System paid ResultSource to purchase these books at retail price in a way that counts toward bestseller sales.

There are so many ways to dislike this marketing plan. Let's take a look at some of the relevant facts and issues.

- It takes 3,000 hardcover sales in one week to make The Wall Street Journal's business bestseller list, and as much as 5,000/week to make The New York Times business bestseller list.

- Bestseller lists do not count bulk sales. Corporations buying their own books and then giving them away is a common example of bulk sales that no longer count toward bestseller lists. However, if 500 unique employees at a corporation use their own accounts to make 500 individual purchases of a book, those would all count toward bestseller sales.

- Neither reporter Trachtenberg nor ResultSource principal Kevin Small would detail what one client called their "secret sauce" for how they get the sales to count toward bestseller lists. I've been in on a few of these campaigns, though, so I'll spill a few details.

• One part of the secret sauce is the way Amazon.com counts bestsellers. I suspect a sale counts if it is a single copy of a title. One way of rigging the sales, then, would be to open hundreds of Amazon accounts for the purpose of ordering a single book on the same day.

• Another part of the sauce likely is that sales of multiple copies of a book will count toward bestseller sales if they are shipped to unique addresses. This would give a company like ResultSource a back door for engineering bestseller status: load up the mailing list and have the retailer send one book to everyone on the list.

• As an Amazon Prime member, shipping is free on many books stocked by Amazon. This dramatically reduces the cost of using Amazon.com to do the fulfillment when mailing out free books.

This Strategy is Expensive

If these sales are made to look like retail sales, they are ringing up at 65% of list price (a typical retail discount). For the book, Prescription for Excellence: Leadership Lessons for Creating a World Class Customer Experience from

UCLA Health System, Amazon shows a list price of $28 and a discounted price of $18.29 (35% off).

It likely cost the UCLA Health System $182,900 to buy 10,000 copies of this book through Amazon — that's before taxes and shipping. It would cost them about $25,000 to have that many copies printed. You're looking at a minimum $100,000 added cost to engineer a one-week appearance on the bestseller list.

Prescription for Excellence sold 13,000 copies the first week and less than 500 copies a week thereafter. In the two years since its publication date, it has sold a total of 28,000 copies (including digital sales). Most likely, more than half the sales of the printed book have been to the UCLA Health System itself.

The UCLA Health System website states they are "owned and operated by the people of California…all 38 million of them." I'm sure the people of California are thrilled to know the UCLA Health System spent twice as much as it would have cost to print and mail these books just to engineer a 7-day appearance on a bestseller list.

Hopefully, the results of their medical studies are not rigged like their appearance on the bestseller lists.

I worked on a campaign to get a book about homelessness into the offices of every U.S. Representative and Senator (535 copies). We considered purchasing the books through Amazon.com and letting them do the fulfillment, but it was one-quarter the cost if we bought them from the publisher and had the publisher's fulfillment center do the shipping.

It doesn't seem right to take money earmarked for the homeless (or for health care) and use it for self-aggrandizement. I can understand lobbying with a book. I've promoted books on immigration reform, health care reform, financial reform, relations between the U.S. and Israel — you name the issue — and I've never seen a client make a huge buy of their own book just to crack the bestseller lists.

Amazon Bestseller Campaign

I have worked with authors who conducted "Amazon

Bestseller Campaigns." I've never produced one myself, but I know how they work. You put together a mailing to, say, 50,000 people, offering incentives if they purchase the client's book on a specific day.

You round up incentives for the mailing with this sort of pitch: "Hey, do you want to be part of a big 50,000-person mailing for your services? I need you to give me something I can give away, such as a free consultation or a white paper or a sample of some kind. And then you have to send the same mailing to your list as everyone else is sending to their lists."

If you get 10 sponsors, and they each have an average of 5,000 names on their mailing list, you have a 50,000-name list and you're mailing will include 10 incentives to purchase the book on the specified day. That's the "Amazon Bestseller Campaign" in a nutshell: bribe people to buy your book on a specific day.

If only the fish were more reliable. There's no guarantee the fish will take the bait and buy on the magic day. Therefore, it's wise for the marketer to set aside a portion of the fee to purchase copies for themselves — to make sure that some sales transpire.

That concept has evolved into ResultSource. Soren Kaplan, the author of Leapfrogging, paid ResultSource $22/copy to buy 2,500 copies of his book the week it debuted. He also paid roughly $10/copy in fees, for a total bestseller campaign cost of about $80,000. Sales have been less than 100 copies/week since the book published.

Amazon Bestseller Party

The problem with engineered bestsellers is, the higher they go, the harder they crash. Amazon bestsellers maybe sustained for only a matter of hours before they plummet like a skydiver with a broken parachute.

It's often easier and less expensive to engineer real sales than fake sales. It does require some creativity, though, which is sadly in short supply. I had a client who once asked me to round-up 20 positive Amazon reviews for his book. I told him my firm doesn't do that. He persisted that he needed to "do something" and did I know a firm that would generate those reviews for him.

"Here's what you do," I said. "You're having a coming out party for your book, right? Many of your family and friends will be there, and they will expect a free copy of your book. You want to be sure you collect a review for every free copy you give away."

"How do I do that," he asked.

"You have an assistant with a laptop or tablet computer open to Amazon.com, and you ask everyone to please take a few moments to share their thoughts about your book on Amazon. If you have booze at the event, you should have no trouble collecting 20 positive reviews."

Call it an Amazon Bestseller Party!

Almost any stupid marketing stunt you can think of, SixEstate can think of three better ones that pass the smell test, won't backfire on your brand, and have a real chance of making a lasting impression with your target audience.

Despite giving away over 10,000 copies of their Prescription for Excellence, the UCLA Health System book has only five reviews at Amazon in two years. There were probably more than five people in the meeting where this marketing campaign was approved. Stay tuned to SixEstate News for more creative ideas about intelligent ways you can establish thought leadership in your field.

Chapter 24

Media Kits and Publicity Planning

By Chris E. Stout

You can be proactive with seeking venues to present. I have spoken at Rotary Clubs, Lyons Clubs, Women's Leadership Groups and the like as well as submitting for professional presentations. It is very tacky to "sell from the stage" but certainly your introduction or printed bio note can mention your book.

I am a big fan of forms, and in my *Getting Started in*

Private Practice book, I created two forms that can help concretize what you may want to consider in developing your planning. So, think about what Media Outlet you'll pitch to, reasons to contact you, any deadlines, your publicity/relevance idea, ways to make your work stand out, and what you need to do to make it happen.

Your Publicity Action Plan

	Media Outlet (Newspaper, Television Station, Etc.)	Reasons To Contact (Event)	Deadline
1.			
2.			
3.			
4.			
5.			
6.			
7.			
8.			

	Publicity Idea	Ways To Make My Work Stand Out	What I Need To Do To Make It Happen
1.			
2.			
3.			
4.			
5.			
6.			
7.			
8.			

Your Presentation Planner

1. What are five topic ideas for presentations you could make within the next six months?

    a. _____
    b. _____
    c. _____
    d. _____
    e. _____

2. Which of your colleagues could you ask to co-present with you? They don't necessarily have to be therapists. For example, you could present a workshop for people who have been downsized and your co-presenter could be a management recruiter. You could focus on maintaining self-esteem and the recruiter could focus on interviewing skills.

    List ideas here:

    _____
    _____
    _____
    _____

3. Which ten organizations can you approach about making a presentation?

Name of organization	Contact Person	Deadline

Your New Business Card

One of the things I also like about CreateSpace books is that I can buy them fairly inexpensively and give them away as a gift. My *Meaningful Productivity* title costs me about $3.00 apiece and depending on the situation, I may provide an important contact or dear friend with a copy. Make sure you have a good bio and contact information in your book for this purpose as well.

Your CreateSpace book, then is book is also your new "brochure" demonstrating quite vividly your expertise and a promotional tool/give-away. You can edit and update as often as you like and print more. It is a nice, passive yet powerful way to promote your brand with the kind words/endorsements you may have on the back cover or as a Foreword.

Media Kits

It is fun to make a media kit. I have a few—different ones for different books, and a general one for multipurpose use. It is a good idea to have nice graphics and be sure to include points as to why an audience would what to hear what you have to say. What follows is one that I used for library talks for *The New Humanitarians*. In it you'll see not only a more full bio, but a helpful to the librarian short introduction. The goal is to make the life of whomever you are sending the Kit to very easy. I created it in Word and save it as a PDF so I would be sure it would look like it should when emailed as an attached file.

Dr. Chris E. Stout
Founding Director
Center for Global Initiatives

Clinical Professor
College of Medicine,
University of Illinois-Chicago

Winner of Three
Humanitarian Awards

CENTER FOR
GLOBAL INITIATIVES

Author of
The New
Humanitarians

Do It Yourself
Humanitarianism

Helping Others Change the World...

Would your patrons like to take a trip around the world—at your library?

Would they like to learn how to change the world?

Would they like to know how those that have founded some of the most successful humanitarian organizations did it?

Now they can with Dr. Chris E. Stout, author of recently published three-volume book-set, *The New Humanitarians: Inspiration, Innovations, and Blueprints for Visionaries.* These books document interviews Dr. Stout conducted with the founders and directors of 45 incredible humanitarian organizations across the globe. In his presentation he tells the stories of their development and how they function today, along with amazing and beautiful slides from around the world.

This hour long inspirational presentation is fast moving and punctuated with humorous stories and anecdotes fit for all ages, driven by Dr. Stout's down-to-earth presentation style.

Don't be surprised if the audience leaves wanting to start their own project as Dr. Stout will provide them with the tools and know-how along with the motivation!

BIOGRAPHY

Speaker Introduction Biography

Dr. Chris Stout is the Founding Director of the Center for Global Initiatives, a Clinical Professor in the College of Medicine at the University of Illinois-Chicago, and author of over 30 books, including his latest 3 volume set, The New Humanitarians: Inspiration, Innovations, and Blueprints for Visionaries. He will be discussing both his Center and his latest books.

Dr. Stout is an inspiring role model who will not only share fascinating stories of his adventuresome, humanitarian service based life, but also discuss ways in which his Center can help support/sponsor the work of other organizations or even help incubate, fund, and launch projects based on an individual's passion to make a true difference in the world, maybe even yours! His leadership mantra is that he accomplished what he did on his own, and now he has a Center to help others do likewise— only faster and better! He calls it "Do It Yourself Humanitarianism."™ It may change you life as well as others!

FULL PROFESSIONAL BIOGRAPHY

Dr. Stout is a licensed clinical psychologist and brings a diverse background perfectly tailored to making the Center for Global Initiatives into a reality. He also is a Clinical Full Professor in the College of Medicine, Department of Psychiatry, a Fellow in the School of Public Health Leadership Institute, and is a Core Faculty at the International Center on Responses to Catastrophes at the University of Illinois, Chicago. He also holds an academic appointment in the Northwestern University Feinberg Medical School, and was a Visiting Professor in the Department of Health Systems Management at Rush University. He served as a NGO Special Representative to the United Nations. He was appointed by the Secretary of the US Department of Commerce to the Board of Examiners for the Baldrige National Quality Award. He holds the distinction of being one of only 100 world-wide leaders appointed to the World Economic Forum's Global Leaders of Tomorrow 2000 – joining the ranks of Tony Blair, Jody Foster, Bill Gates, R. J. Rowling, and Lance Armstrong, and he was an Invited Faculty at the Annual Meeting in Davos. He was invited by the Club de Madrid and Safe-Democracy to serve on the Madrid-11 Countering Terrorism Task Force.

Dr. Stout is a Fellow in the American Psychological Association, past-President of the Illinois Psychological Association, and is a Distinguished Practitioner in the National Academies of Practice. Dr. Stout has published or presented over 300 papers and 30 books. His works have been translated into 8 languages. He has lectured across the nation and internationally in 19 countries, and visited 6 continents and over 75 countries. He is the 2004 winner of the American Psychological Association's International Humanitarian Award, the 2006 recipient of the Illinois Psychological Association's Humanitarian Award and the 2008 recipient of the Psychologists for Social Responsibility's Humanitarian Award.

He founded a kindergarten for AIDS orphaned children in Tanzania. He is a signatory to the UN's 50th Anniversary of the Universal Declaration of Human Rights. Dr. Stout was educated at Purdue, The University of Chicago's Graduate School of Business, and Forest Institute. At Harvard Medical School he was a Fellow in neuro-developmental behavioral pediatrics. He was awarded "Distinguished Alumni of the Year from Purdue University" in 1991.

He also produced award winning Public Service Announcements. He has been interviewed on many radio, cable, local, and national television programs (e.g., CNBC, CNN, WGN, NBC, PBS, NPR, Chicago Tonight, Oprah, Eye On Harvard, et al), and by numerous publications (Time, Chicago Tribune, The Wall Street Journal, New York Times, USA Today, Modern Healthcare, Associated Press...).

PRESENTATION IDEAS

IDEAS TO ENGAGE YOUR PATRONS

"How to live your dream of making a difference."

"How to have a legacy of making the world a better place."

"Tools and methods of creating your own non-for-profit."

"Where do you want to go? What do you want to do? We can make it happen."

"Learn how to change the world."

"Learn how some of the best humanitarian organizations do what they do."

"Get the inside scoop on how the best humanitarian organizations started."

"You can become a Hew Humanitarian."

"Making a difference in the world—Yes, you can."

Synopsis of The New Humanitarians

Welcome to a trip around the world. You will travel to six continents, led by men and women of various ages and backgrounds. Be warned, you may go to some fairly desperate places, but they all have a seed of hope. You will not be traveling as a tourist, but rather as an activist with more than three dozen organizations—each one incredible.

Each chapter is a story, a story of need, of response, and of accomplishment. They are all at once different, but yet the same as being an inspirational account demonstrating the power of the individual triumphant over the challenges of poverty, illness, conflict, or a litany of injustices. My friend, Jonathan Granoff, President of the Global Security Institute, said of the project that it is a counter to the pervasive "pornography of the trivial" that infects much of what is in print these days. I suspect he is correct.

While many of us are content in helping various causes by writing checks of support or perhaps even volunteering, the individuals profiled herein preferred to actually start their own organizations—to enact their passionate interests. So, therein was the idea that crystallized the concept for this New Humanitarians project. I wanted to find out what makes these New Humanitarians tick and how their brainchildren worked. Now, through this three volume set, readers can, too.

In developing the Center for Global Initiatives, I came to realize that while there are many successful, ground-breaking models that already exist world-wide, there really isn't a blueprint or a how-to on the subject. While this is most likely due to the uniqueness of the organizations and their leadership examined herein, as well as their idiosyncratic approach to conducting their work, it is my hope that this book-set will nevertheless provide readers a unique behind-the-scenes glimpse of the organizations and offer incredibly valuable insights, present insider experiences, and give advice that few would ever have access to from one organization, let alone from more than forty of the best-of-the-best.

I have been fortunate to have had the rare and heady opportunity to have worked with some of the most innovative humanitarian organizations in the world, or to have collaborated with their incredibly talented founders/directors. It is my experiences with these incredible people that led to my idea for this book project. Many have more skin-in-the-game.

Looks Who's talking About The New Humanitarians and What they are Saying...

"All of us aspire to someday "make a real difference" in the world yet, caught up in our own day-to-day personal crises and seemingly pressing obligations, very few of us ever fulfill this important human dream Chris Stout is a world class humanitarian who has taken the time to vividly explore the inside world of those who have succeeded Perhaps with this new appreciation for how to succeed, more of us will eventually fulfill our own personal quest to make the world just a little bit better."

Pat DeLeon, Ph.D., M.P.H., JD, Past President of the American Psychological Association

"Stout's stories of social innovators in The New Humanitarians are inspiring and instructive -- helpful to anyone who wants to participate in building a better world."

David Bornstein, author, How to Change The World: Social Entrepreneurs and the Power of New Ideas, and The Price of a Dream, and has written for The Atlantic Monthly, The New York Times, New York Newsday, and other major publications.

"Usually we think it takes someone extraordinary to do something of great value—a Gandhi or a King In fact, the people profiled in these volumes are just like most of us—nobodies to start with, who became somebodies because they answered a call. The moral here may be that if we hear that "still small voice," act on it. It can make a difference, including just supporting any of these organizations at any level, or one like them."

John Steiner, Co-founder, The National Commons and Chair, the Transpartisan Center

"Poverty takes many forms, from lack of health care and the most basic education, to vulnerability to the abuse of others. Where governments and multilateral agencies are falling short, concerned individuals have been racing forward with creative solutions like white blood cells addressing infections. This is one of the most powerful movements at work in the world today. Chris Stout is shining a bright light on their critically important work."

Welford Welch, Author, The Tactics of Hope - How Social Entrepreneurs Are Changing Our World

"We learn by our own experiences and by living the experiences of others through stories. We are human because of our connectedness with other humans. What Chris has done in The New Humanitarians is to capture and share in a compelling way the inspirational stories of people who are making a real difference to others; people who are leading beyond self-interest. Just think if we all did that…"

Fields Wicker-Miurin is the co-founder and Partner of Leaders' Quest, former Chief Financial and Strategy Officer of the London Stock Exchange, Non-Executive Director of the CDC Group plc, the UK's development finance institution, and a Governor of King's College London.

Ad hoc Media Kit

I was recently asked to be interviewed for a radio show on *Getting Better at Private Practice.* What follows is that I sent in an email in response.

Radio Show Questions for Dr Chris Stout,

author of ***Getting Better at Private Practice*** (Wiley, 2012).

<u>Website</u>: DrChrisStout.com

<u>BIO</u>: Dr. Stout is the author of over 35 books including Amazon best sellers such as ***Getting Better at Private Practice*** and ***Getting Started in Private Practice.*** He frequently speaks lectures on practice development issues and privately consults to practice owners. He has vast experience with start-ups in for- and not-for-profit organizations. He is a licensed clinical psychologist, Fellow in the American Psychological Association, and Past-President of the Illinois Psychological Association. He was named a Global Leader of Tomorrow by the World Economic Forum and was a faculty at their famous Annual Meeting in Davos. He has been honored for his

international humanitarian work via four awards for such and most recently was given an honorary doctorate from the Purdue School of Engineering.

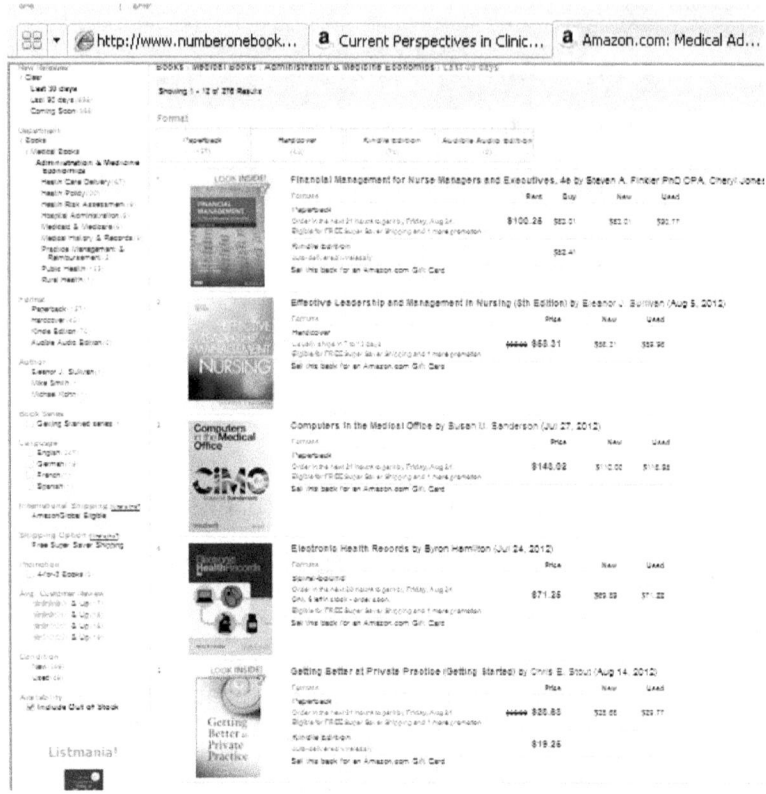

At 3 weeks out *Getting Better at Private Practice* was ranked at #5 in its category on Amazon!

Interview Questions

1. What was the impetus for your "Getting Started..." books with Wiley?

2. You have a remarkable track record of publishing—both best-selling books and in peer reviewed journals. How does someone "get started" in in publishing?

3. You talk about an "elevator pitch" in your lectures and books, what is that?

4. What is the single best tip you can give our listeners today to help them with their practice or marketing their business?

5. What are the worst things you have seen when marketing's gone bad?

   6. You have been pretty prolific in start-ups, writing, and various other activities, what's next?

   # # #

What follows is the flyer Wiley developed for *Getting Started in Private Practice*. It gives you an idea of how to construct you own and what others on the receiving end are used to seeing from the big publishing houses.

As Wiley is also quite involved in professional meetings, they cannot attend all the ones their authors may. So they offer these helpful tips that I wanted to share and help you understand what support a large publisher can offer.

WHAT CAN YOU DO TO PROMOTE YOUR BOOK AT A CONFERENCE THAT WILEY IS NOT ATTENDING

Once your book is published, you may attend a conference that is not on Wiley's schedule but is an ideal market for your book. Each year we get hundreds of requests from authors asking us to market their books at small or medium sized conferences. It has be our experience that it not cost-effective to devote our energy and resources to support these efforts. Finally, we realize significantly better results focusing our attention on bulk sales, large reseller programs, channel development, and market research.

- To promote your book at a conference or presentation we will provide you with flyers that you can distribute. Please contact us four-to-six weeks before the event to ensure the flyers will be produced in a timely fashion. Email requests to wiley.com

- If you are selling or displaying books at a conference,

you will need to arrange the logistics such as table rental, display hours, location, and other details.

• If you decide to display your books at a conference or to order books for resale at a conference, contact Joe Blow in the Wiley Sales Department (Email: @wiley.com or call 555-555-5555).

• If you would like to work with a regional bookstore or conference organizer to sell your books at a conference, contact Sally Joe (@wiley.com) or Joe Black (@wiley.com) who will supply you with a list of Wiley agency accounts that are organized by states. The agency accounts have agreed to be approached for onsite local conference selling opportunities. You can call or FAX these accounts and give detailed information about the dates, location, and name of the conference coordinator. We typically need a minimum of 8 weeks' notice in order to process your request.

What follows are some general tips from Wiley that you may also find helpful in your promotional efforts.

Book Promotion Tips

You can play a very important role in promoting your

forthcoming book. No doubt you have countless colleagues and clients whom you can contact to help in this promotion and, thereby, increase sales. You may have access to association lists, know influential individuals in your field, or be affiliated with institutions or organizations interested in bulk purchases. Keep in mind that these contacts will be much more receptive to you than to a publisher.

The following are suggestions of ways you can tap into your own professional network to help promote your book and greatly enhance our marketing efforts:

- **Mail book flyers to personal contacts**. Upon request, we will provide you with flyers (essentially, a one-page advertisement of your book with ordering information) that you can mail/distribute to your colleagues, clients, workshop attendees, or anyone that you know who may be interested in your book. Mailed with a personal note or letter, this approach is very successful in producing additional sales.

- **Book reviews**. People in the media pay more attention to a book that they receive from someone they know than from a publisher. If you have any contacts in the media – whether an editor at a scholarly journal or newspaper reporter – send them a copy of your book for review. Again, a personal note from you and a copy of your book's promotional flyer helps capture the attention of book review editors.

- **Article adoption**. Develop articles from your book and place them in publications with large circulations, and be sure to include order information from Wiley.

- **Bulk sales and textbook adoption**. Contact people you know at universities, corporations, and associations who make buying decisions. We can send complimentary copies of your book to these pre-qualified sales leads.

- **Conferences, speaking engagements, and workshops**. At your upcoming conferences, speaking engagements or workshops, you can make arrangements to have your book displayed at the event.

- **Publicity**. If you are affiliated with a university, involve your public relations and/or alumni office in the promotion of your book. Learn if any of the organizations with which you are associated offer PR services and utilize their expertise.

PRAEGER

We are delighted to welcome you to Praeger!

This kit is intended to introduce you to the Marketing staff and to explain th basic processes that take place to promote your book to the marketplace, libraries, professors, schools and other venues.

Please use your judgment to identify the right person to best address your query. In general, you should contact your editor first.

Contact:

- **Your Editor** to get official publication dates, contract concerns, websit copy changes, ebooks, personal publicity efforts and manuscript issue
- **Customer Service** to purchase copies of your book with your author discount orders@greenwood.com, call 800-225-5800 or fax 603-431-221
- **Carol Gudzik** for book purchases for your planned events Carol.Gudzik@greenwood.com
- **Kathy Barrett** for sales, availability and inventory information Kathy.Barrett@greenwood.com

We are excited to be working with you and want your book to be as much of success as possible.

Sincerely,

Karin Kuczynski-Holmgren
Senior Marketing Manager, Praeger
Karin.Holmgren@greenwood.com

This is the packet Praeger provides to authors to help develop an integrated marketing push. This is just the cover, but if you'd like a free PDF of it go to the private link at:

https://www.slideshare.net/secret/j8fK9qlvQGMXfland use the password: StoutOnPublishing

$peaking Engagements

You may find yourself invited to speak at a conference, congratulations! Now, you may have some ideas in your mind how this will work, and they may have something quite different—does travel mean just the airplane or the taxies back and forth from the airport? Food *and* hotel? Actual costs or a daily *per diem*…? These are all the things than can help you decide if it's worth it for you to go. Also, it may be worth it even if there are no fees or expenses covered if there is a strategic benefit for you.

It can also be awkward to ask such questions. So I developed this form that I edit as need be in a Word file format and then send along to the host. It makes for great clarity for both parties and peace of mind for you! Feel free to use mine and edit as need be! The complete version appears in *Getting Started in Private Practice.*

Your letterhead

Professional Speaking Agreement

It is my goal to help you have a successful meeting. Please help me contribute to your success by completing this brief questionnaire. Thank you!

General Issues:

What issues does your industry currently face?

_____
_____
_____

What global or internal problems need to be addressed?

_____
_____
_____

What type of message do you want me to send? Motivational? Inspirational? Educational?

_____
_____
_____

Title of the meeting: _____
Other speakers: _____
Other topics and titles:

_____
_____
_____

How would you describe the "personality" of the audience?

_____

Technical Details:

Where is the presentation (venue name)? _____
City: _____ State/Country: _____
When is the presentation: (day, date, time)? _____
How long is my presentation? _____
What is the nature of your meeting? _____
Who will be attending? _____

You may also want to get your name out in services that help place speakers. Here is one that I use:

http://www.wcspeakers.com

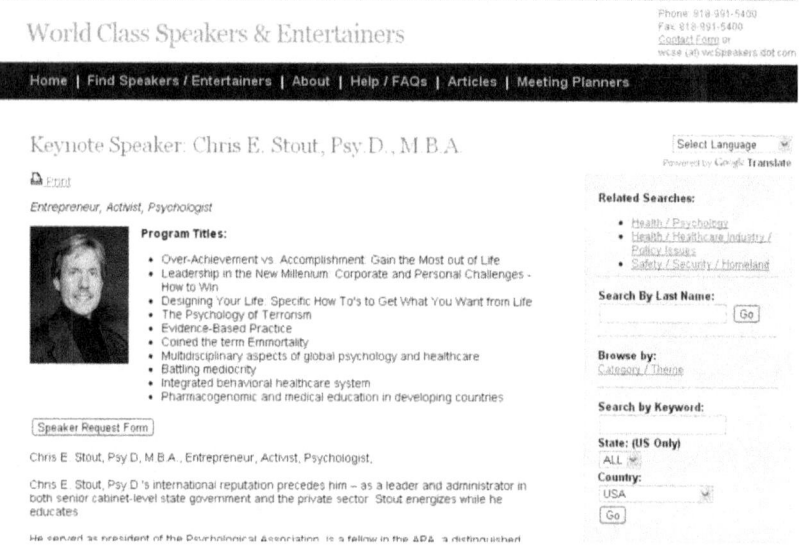

Appendix A

Great phrases to sprinkle in and spice up your prose, tweak a bland sentence, or help break through writer's block. This is my organic, self-organizing thesaurus that usually helps me come off like Ayn Rand and William F. Buckley's love-child with my facile and oh so clever use of big-words.

- ☐ Plastic sloganeering

- ☐ Scatological exhaustion

- ☐ Oily-voweled apparatchiks

- ☐ Pretzelized political correctness

- ☐ Bullying nihilism herniates

- ☐ Somnambulant giant

- ☐ Refugees: Freud, Einstein, Solti, Kissinger, Picasso

- ☐ The premise on which you base the question is wrong

- ☐ Supported by little/nothing but inexperience

- ☐ …created a perfect frustration machine…
- ☐ Idiosyncratic talents
- ☐ Cutting-edge auteurs
- ☐ Radical ventures
- ☐ Anarchic, critical thrust
- ☐ Melancholy isolate inhabit
- ☐ Potent chimera
- ☐ Febrile randiness
- ☐ Bully's Bluff
- ☐ Bully pulpit
- ☐ Dried-out spoor
- ☐ Detailed exegesis
- ☐ Academic claqueur
- ☐ Felicitous articulation
- ☐ Liberal shibboleth
- ☐ Pandering insipidity
- ☐ Hoi polloi
- ☐ Sacerdotal Figure
- ☐ Lips to celebrity breeches
- ☐ Con amore
- ☐ Results over protocol
- ☐ Man who tells the fireplace to make him warm, and THEN he'll put in some wood
- ☐ Fool's errand

- ☐ Goofy, witless innocents
- ☐ Comfort zone of smirking condescension
- ☐ Sleight-of-hand
- ☐ Sees the world as full of mostly useful idiots
- ☐ If "Smith's" definition (of____) was baggy and capacious, then "Jones's" definitions were filigree to an overwrought fault.
- ☐ Feel superior to their own foot soldiers in the proletarian heartland
- ☐ No need to distinguish truth or detail
- ☐ Moral carpet-bombing from 10,000 feet
- ☐ Dark doppelganger
- ☐ To flourish, to opine, to be important
- ☐ Frothed up like a cappuccino laced with arsenic
- ☐ Keep behind the curtain of blood
- ☐ Sophistry (subtly deceptive reasoning or argumentation) masquerading as protest
- ☐ Profligate Ways
- ☐ Rage unhinged from fact
- ☐ Preachy nonalignment
- ☐ Cordon of comfort
- ☐ Infantile rebellion
- ☐ Schizoid detachment
- ☐ Feral charisma

- ☐ Scandalous transgressiveness
- ☐ Austere visual beauty
- ☐ Hybrid aesthetic
- ☐ Dankly anhidrotic
- ☐ Catastrophic injury
- ☐ Blitzkrieg and panzers
- ☐ Libidinous stare
- ☐ Modus vivendi
- ☐ Entrench the core malaise
- ☐ Moribund marriage
- ☐ Exuberant promiscuity
- ☐ Anhedonic milieu
- ☐ Anomic present
- ☐ Serpentine grid
- ☐ Hegelian hocus-pocus
- ☐ Aesthetic crank turned _____
- ☐ Carting in rent-a-radical to indoctrinate them in the theater of outrage
- ☐ Pyrrhic Victory - a victory/success @ too great a cost
- ☐ Pixie Titan
- ☐ Desolate hedonism
- ☐ Liberal apostasy
- ☐ Stochastic conjectural
- ☐ éminence grise

- ☐ Machine esthetics
- ☐ Tyranny of the majority
- ☐ Inchoate sentiments
- ☐ Monotony of thought
- ☐ Independence of mind
- ☐ Autodidact self-assurance competence
- ☐ Evangelistic Tome
- ☐ Evangelical fervor
- ☐ Capra on acid
- ☐ Crisis of Conscience
- ☐ Standard of Utility
- ☐ Idiot savant
- ☐ Jaded to the Point Of Inertia
- ☐ Ontogeny Recapitulates Phylogeny
- ☐ Pregnant Remarks
- ☐ Res Ipsa Loquitur (The Fact speaks for itself)
- ☐ Asphyxiated with emotion (Like Nascent (Beginning to Develop) Oxygen, exists only for a short duration)
- ☐ Indecent alacrity (cheerful readiness; briskness)
- ☐ Double entendre
- ☐ Particular gravity & depth
- ☐ Peculiar gravity & depth
- ☐ Straight-Jacketed idealog
- ☐ Moral Aphasia

- [ ] Idea Deficit Disorder
- [ ] Innovation Deficit Disorder
- [ ] Ratchet of progress
- [ ] Ultimate prosthesis
- [ ] Piatefic and selfish
- [ ] Gordian Knot
- [ ] Pyrrhic victory
- [ ] Potent Logarithm
- [ ] Biblical cadence
- [ ] Clamorous sycophant
- [ ] Promethean power
- [ ] Unleash a Niagara
- [ ] Unique alchemy
- [ ] Protean monster
- [ ] Fetishistic prattling
- [ ] Ad homenum attack
- [ ] Gravitational center of opinion
- [ ] Tinkerish knack
- [ ] Individual strength and civic virtue.
- [ ] Tempest in a tea pot
- [ ] Reckless Abandon
- [ ] Apollonian law to Dionysian spirit
- [ ] Theorists, Critics, & Commentators
- [ ] Panoramas of opportunity

- ☐ Claustrophobic testimonies
- ☐ Multifarious carrels of fact
- ☐ Diurnal world
- ☐ Regnant superstitions
- ☐ Malthusian odds
- ☐ A heartwarming dishonesty
- ☐ Credulousness and Detachment
- ☐ Seeing and blind at the same time
- ☐ A license to say the unspeakable
- ☐ My stomach tightened with terror & hope
- ☐ A kinship of misfits
- ☐ A license to speak full throated
- ☐ Curious contradiction
- ☐ Provincial Foolishness
- ☐ Lame satire
- ☐ Hypocrisy was the order of the hour
- ☐ World containing smile
- ☐ The iron logic of _____
- ☐ An act of contrition
- ☐ Speaking in many disguises
- ☐ Expressionless tranquility
- ☐ A withering parody
- ☐ Skidding into oblivion
- ☐ Imagination Deficit Disorder

- ☐ Moral Aphasia
- ☐ Bell the cat
- ☐ Doing the difficult
- ☐ Abstract vagueness
- ☐ Malicious prosecution
- ☐ Modesty and patience are taken as signs of weakness
- ☐ Facts are stubborn things
- ☐ Peripheral-Vision (to imply having "vision" but not the typical focused vision of a visionary person)
- ☐ Tyranny of the majority
- ☐ Lingua franca (language of the group)
- ☐ Lumpkin pipsqueak - low class, shiftless
- ☐ "Falls in a hail of pedantry"
- ☐ Indiscriminate possibilism
- ☐ Archly preconscious dialogue
- ☐ Gnomic exchanges
- ☐ Retrospective dystopia
- ☐ Retrospective myopia
- ☐ ...lacks a shiver of prophecy
- ☐ Fools' errand
- ☐ Red herring
- ☐ Straw man
- ☐ Agile mind
- ☐ Job's comforter: a person who discourages and/or

depresses while seemingly giving comfort and consolation

- ☐ Live with intensity
- ☐ Don't live easy, but well
- ☐ Customers run your business, not you.
- ☐ From success to significance
- ☐ Done Beats Perfect
- ☐ Tolerating Obsolescence & Discouraging Innovation
- ☐ Weapons of mass potential
- ☐ Technological agnostics
- ☐ Immensely old young man
- ☐ Episcopal dignity
- ☐ Machine esthetics
- ☐ Double-Domed
- ☐ Ineffectual Solipsist
- ☐ Abstract vagueness
- ☐ Muster the energy, dedication, and tenacity to...
- ☐ "bla-bla" is a tactic not a strategy
- ☐ Abundantly obvious
- ☐ Artificial distinction
- ☐ Trenchant question
- ☐ Familiar bromides
- ☐ Totem of real inspiration
- ☐ Lightening rod of...

- ☐ Howls of dinosaurs
- ☐ Wunderkinds new clothes
- ☐ Embellished by poetical ornament
- ☐ Beneath the tousled, low key approach is a boiling drive
- ☐ Spurious intimacy with the great
- ☐ Hard work and frenzied industry
- ☐ Autistic despot
- ☐ Provincial vs. radical perspective/approach
- ☐ X is simply a different point of view
- ☐ Corporate excellence from individual excellence on behalf of the patient
- ☐ Corseted by laws or Corseted by _____ (whatever restrictive)
- ☐ The almost palpable power of _____
- ☐ _____ trumpeting its fraudulence
- ☐ _____ like a fiend
- ☐ Counter fear/popular hysteria
- ☐ Pestilent influence
- ☐ A whiff of brimstone and a touch of Proust
- ☐ A Roman candle of feminist enthusiasm
- ☐ Too busy driving to stop for gas/too busy sawing down a tree to sharpen the saw
- ☐ Familiar bromides
- ☐ Complexity and ambiguity of our positions

☐   Champions (zealots), copy cats, and walk-ins

☐   An occasional shivering truth that flies centrifugally out of its centripetal whirl,

☐ Mephistophelian bargain/offer - Devil's representative Mephistopheles appears. He makes a bargain with Faust: Mephistopheles will serve Faust with his magic powers for a term of years, but at the end of the term, the Devil will claim Faust's soul and Faust will be eternally damned. During the term, Faust makes use of Mephistopheles in various ways. In many versions of the story, Mephistopheles helps him to seduce a beautiful and innocent girl, usually named Gretchen, who is destroyed. However, Gretchen's naive innocence saves her in the end and she enters Heaven. However, Faust is irrevocably corrupted, and when the term ends, the Devil carries him off to Hell.

Appendix B

Great Vocab

- **Absent** - not present; missing; not existent; lacking; exhibiting or feeling inattentiveness.

- **Acquiescent** - Disposed or willing to acquiesce; disposed to acquiesce or consent tacitly.

- **Acrimonious** - Biting Sharpness of language or feeling

- **Acrocephalic** - pointy-head

- **Ad infinitum** - a Latin phrase meaning "to infinity" or "forevermore".

- **Adjudicate** - Settle Judicially

- **Adjunct** - Something attached to another in a dependent or subordinate position; A person associated with another in a subordinate or auxiliary capacity; Attached to a faculty or staff in a temporary or auxiliary capacity; A clause or phrase added to a sentence that, while not essential to the sentence's structure, amplifies its meaning.

- **Adoxography** - good writing about a trivial subject

- **Aegis** - Shield, sponsorship; The modern concept of doing something "under someone's aegis" means doing something under the protection of a powerful, knowledgeable, or benevolent source.

- **Amalgamate** - To combine into a unified or integrated whole; unite; To mix or alloy (a metal) with mercury.

- **Amateurish** - Characteristic of an amateur; not professional; lacking professional skill or expertise.

- **Ambiance** - The special atmosphere or mood created by a particular environment.

- **Amen** - Used at the end of a prayer or a statement to express assent or approval.

- **Anarchy** - Absence of any form of political authority; Political disorder and confusion; Absence of any cohesive principle, such as a common standard or purpose.

- **Anathema** - a curse or someone/thing cursed/disliked

- **Anodyne** - Capable of soothing or eliminating pain; Relaxing.

- **Anomalous/Anomaly -** 2 theories don't jibe

- **Antechamber** - room forming an entrance

- **Aperçu** - A discerning perception, an insight; A short outline or summary; a synopsis.

- **Aplomb** - complete self-assured composure

- **Apnea** - Temporary absence or cessation of breathing; suspension of breathing.

- **Apropos** - Being at once opportune and to the point; At an appropriate time; opportunely; By the way; incidentally; With regard to; concerning.

- **Archaic** - Of, relating to, or characteristic of a much earlier, often more primitive period, especially one that develops into a classical stage of civilization; No longer current or applicable; antiquated; Of, relating to, or characteristic of words and language that were once in regular use but are now relatively rare and suggestive of an earlier style or period.

- **Archetype** - An original model or type after which other similar things are patterned; a prototype; An ideal example of a type; quintessence; In Jungian psychology, an inherited pattern of thought or symbolic imagery derived from the past collective experience and present in the individual unconscious.

- **Architectonic** - Of or relating to architecture or design; Having qualities, such as design and structure, that are characteristic of architecture; Of or relating to the scientific systematization of knowledge.

- **Arrhythmic** - Lacking rhythm or regularity of rhythm.

- **Arrogant** - Having or displaying a sense of overbearing self-worth or self-importance; Marked by or arising from a feeling or assumption of one's superiority toward others.

- **Articulate -** Endowed with the power of speech; Composed of distinct, meaningful syllables or words, as human speech; Expressing oneself easily in clear and effective language; Characterized by the use of clear, expressive language; Consisting of sections united by joints; jointed.

- **Artifact** - An object produced or shaped by human craft, especially a tool, weapon, or ornament of archaeological or historical interest; Something viewed as a product of human conception or agency rather than an inherent element; A structure or feature not normally present but visible as a result of an external agent or action, such as one seen in a microscopic specimen after fixation, or in an image produced by radiology or electrocardiography; An inaccurate observation, effect, or result, especially one resulting from the technology used in scientific investigation or from experimental error.

- **Assailed** - To attack with or as if with violent blows;

assault; To attack verbally, as with ridicule or censure; To trouble; beset.

- **Autodidact** - a self-taught person

- **Avatar** - The incarnation of a Hindu deity, especially Vishnu, in human or animal form; An embodiment, as of a quality or concept; an archetype; A temporary manifestation or aspect of a continuing entity.

- **Avuncular** - Of or having to do with an uncle; Regarded as characteristic of an uncle, especially in benevolence or tolerance.

- **Awash** - washed by the sea; in such a position or way as to be covered with or as if with water.

- **Bastardization** - To lower in quality or character; debase; To declare or prove (someone) to be a bastard.

- **Beneficent** - Characterized by or performing acts of kindness or charity; Producing benefit; beneficial.

- **Betoken** - To be or give a sign or portent of; to give evidence of; indicate.

- **Bourgeois** - A person belonging to the middle class; A person whose attitudes and behavior are marked by conformity to the standards and conventions of the middle class; In Marxist theory, a member of the property-owning class; a capitalist; Held to be preoccupied with respectability and material values.

- **Bricolage** - build it yourself

- **Cakewalk** - Something easily accomplished; A 19th-century public entertainment among African Americans in which walkers performing the most accomplished or amusing steps won cakes as prizes; A strutting dance, often performed in minstrel shows.

- **Calamity** - An event that brings terrible loss, lasting distress, or severe affliction; a disaster; Dire distress resulting from loss or tragedy.

- **Calcified** - To make or become stony or chalky by deposition of calcium salts; To make or become inflexible and unchanging.

- **Caliber** - the diameter of a circular section; Degree of worth; quality.

- **Candid** - Free from prejudice; impartial; Characterized by openness and sincerity of expression; unreservedly straightforward; Not posed or rehearsed.

- **Candor** - Frankness or sincerity of expression; openness; Freedom from prejudice; impartiality.

- **Carte blanche** - Unrestricted power to act at one's own discretion; unconditional authority.

- **Cassandras** - cursed to know the future, but cannot change it

- **Cavalier** - A gallant or chivalrous man, especially one serving as escort to a woman of high social position; a gentleman; A mounted soldier; a knight; Showing arrogant or offhand disregard; dismissive.

- **Caveat** - A warning or caution; A qualification or explanation; A formal notice filed by an interested party with a court or officer, requesting the postponement of a proceeding until the filer is heard.

- **Cede** - To surrender possession of, especially by treaty; To yield; grant.

- **Chameleon** - A person who changes their opinions or behavior according to the situation.

- **Chasm** - A deep, steep-sided opening in the earth's surface; an abyss or gorge; A sudden interruption of continuity; a gap; A pronounced difference of opinion, interests, or loyalty.

- **Childish** - Of, relating to, or suitable for a child or childhood; Marked by or indicating a lack of maturity; puerile; Not complicated; simple; Affected mentally by old age; senile

- **Chrestomathy** - A selection of literary passages, usually by one author; An anthology used in studying a language.

- **Circumlocutions** - The use of unnecessarily wordy and indirect language; Evasion in speech or writing; A roundabout expression.

- **Circumvent** - To surround (an enemy, for example); enclose or entrap; To go around; bypass; To avoid or get around by artful maneuvering.

- **Cloistered** - A covered walk with an open colonnade on one side, running along the walls of buildings that face a quadrangle; A place, especially a monastery or convent, devoted to religious seclusion.

- **"Coffee-Table"** - implying an emphasis on appearance and an underlying lack of seriousness.

- **Cogency** - Power to compel/constrain

- **Colloquialism** - Colloquial style or quality; A colloquial expression.

- **Collude** - To act together secretly to achieve a fraudulent, illegal, or deceitful purpose; conspire; to conspire together, esp in planning a fraud; connive.

- **Coming-of-age** - the attainment of prominence, respectability, recognition, or maturity.

- **Compulsion** - the act of compelling or the state of being compelled; something that compels; a strong, usu. irresistible impulse to perform an act, esp. one that is irrational or contrary to one's will.

- **Conceit** - A favorable and especially unduly high opinion of one's own abilities or worth; An ingenious or witty turn of phrase or thought; A fanciful poetic image, especially an elaborate or exaggerated comparison; an elaborate, fanciful metaphor, esp. of a strained or far-fetched nature.

- **Concomitant** - Occurring or existing concurrently; attendant; One that occurs or exists concurrently with another.

- **Concuss** - To injure by concussion.

- **Conflate** - to bring together; meld or fuse; to combine (two variant texts, for example) into one whole.

- **Confound** - To cause to become confused or perplexed; To fail to distinguish; mix up; To make (something bad) worse; To cause to be ashamed; abash; To frustrate.

- **Conspicuous** - Easy to notice; obvious; Attracting attention, as by being unusual or remarkable; noticeable.

- **Constellated** - ≈ situated

- **Contagion** - transmission of an influence on the mind or emotions

- **Contempt** - The feeling or attitude of regarding someone or something as inferior, base, or worthless; scorn; The state of being despised or dishonored; disgrace; Open disrespect or willful disobedience of the authority of a court of law or legislative body.

- **Contempt** - The feeling or attitude of regarding someone or something as inferior, base, or worthless; scorn; The state of being despised or dishonored; disgrace; Open disrespect or willful disobedience of the authority of a court of law or legislative body.

- **Conventions** - A formal meeting of members, representatives, or delegates, as of a political party, fraternal society, profession, or industry; The body of persons attending such an assembly; General agreement on or acceptance of certain practices or attitudes.

- **Conversely** - To engage in a spoken exchange of thoughts, ideas, or feelings; talk; To be familiar; associate; Spoken interchange of thoughts and feelings; conversation.

- **Credulity** - disposition to believe something on little evidence; gullibility

- **Cynic** - a person who doesn't want to be disappointed again

- **Deadening** - Material used for soundproofing.

- **Decorum** - Appropriateness of behavior or conduct; propriety; a requirement of correct behaviour in polite society.

- **Demagogy** - The character or practices of a demagogue; demagoguery; the methods or practices of a demagogue.

- **Demigod** - A male being, often the offspring of a god and a mortal, who has some but not all of the powers of a god; An inferior deity; a minor god; A deified man; A person who is highly honored or revered.

- **Deracinate** - pull up by roots

- **Desideratum** - criteria

- **Devoid** - Completely lacking; destitute or empty; not

possessing; totally lacking; destitute.

- **Diatribe** - a bitter, abusive denunciation or criticism.

- **Diatribe** - Angry Criticism; Violent attack in speech or writing

- **Didactic** - Intended to instruct; Morally instructive; Inclined to teach or moralize excessively.

- **Dilettante** - person with superficial interest in art or branch of knowledge

- **Diminution** - The act or process of diminishing; a lessening or reduction; The resulting reduction; decrease; Statement of a theme in notes of lesser duration, usually one-half, of the original.

- **Discourse** - Verbal expression in speech or writing; Verbal exchange; conversation; A formal, lengthy discussion of a subject, either written or spoken; Archaic The process or power of reasoning.

- **Discourse** - Verbal expression in speech or writing; Verbal exchange; conversation; A formal, lengthy discussion of a subject, either written or spoken; The process or power of reasoning.

- **Discursion** - The act of discoursing or reasoning; range, as from thought to thought.

- **Disquiet** - To deprive of peace or rest; trouble; Absence of peace or rest; anxiety; Uneasy; restless.

- **Dogmatic** - Relating to, characteristic of, or resulting from dogma; Characterized by an authoritative, arrogant assertion of unproved or un-provable principles.

- **Doppelgänger** - A ghostly double of a living person, especially one that haunts its fleshly counterpart.

- **Dread** - To be in terror of; To anticipate with alarm, distaste, or reluctance; To hold in awe or reverence; To be very afraid; Profound fear; terror; An object of fear, awe, or reverence.

- **Éclat** - Great brilliance, as of performance or achievement; Conspicuous success; Great acclamation or applause; Notoriety; scandal.

- **Effete** - Depleted of vitality, force, or effectiveness; exhausted; Marked by self-indulgence, triviality, or decadence; Over refined; effeminate; No longer productive; infertile.

- **Egalitarian** - Affirming, promoting, or characterized by belief in equal political, economic, social, and civil rights for all people; of, relating to, or upholding the doctrine of the equality of mankind and the desirability of political, social, and economic equality.

- **Eggheadism** - Smarty-Pants-Ed-Ness

- **Élan** - Enthusiastic vigor and liveliness; Distinctive style or flair.

- **Elucidate -** To make clear or plain, especially by

explanation; clarify; To give an explanation that serves to clarify.

- **Emancipation** - The act or an instance of emancipating; The condition of being emancipated.

- **Engaging** - Charming; attractive

- **Ennobling** - To make noble; To confer nobility upon

- **Ensemble** - A unit or group of complementary parts that contribute to a single effect; A work for two or more vocalists or instrumentalists; all the parts of something considered together and in relation to the whole.

- **Entropy** - a function of thermodynamic variables, as temperature or pressure, that is a measure of the energy that is not available for work in a thermodynamic process; a measure of the loss of information in a transmitted signal; a hypothetical tendency for the universe to attain a state of maximum homogeneity in which all matter is at a uniform temperature; a state of disorder, as in a social system, or a hypothetical tendency toward such a state.

- **Ephemeral** - Lasting for a markedly brief time; Living or lasting only for a day, as certain plants or insects do.

- **Ephemeral** - Lasting for a markedly brief time; Living or lasting only for a day, as certain plants or insects do; A markedly short-lived thing.

- **Epigone** - A second-rate imitator or follower, especially of an artist or a philosopher; an undistinguished imitator, follower, or successor of an important writer, painter, etc.

- **Epiphany** - (Christianity / Ecclesiastical Terms) the manifestation of a supernatural or divine reality; any moment of great or sudden revelation.

- **Epistemology** - Theory Of knowledge

- **Epoch** - A particular period of history, especially one considered remarkable or noteworthy; A notable event that marks the beginning of such a period; A unit of geologic time that is a division of a period; Astronomy An instant in time that is arbitrarily selected as a point of reference.

- **Equitable** - Marked by or having equity; impartial or reasonable; fair; just; recognized in a court of equity only, as claims, rights, etc.

- **Escalate** - To increase, enlarge, or intensify; To increase in intensity or extent; to increase or be increased in extent, intensity, or magnitude.

- **Eschew** - To avoid; shun; to abstain or keep away from.

- **Ethos** - The disposition, character, or fundamental values peculiar to a specific person, people, culture, or movement.

- **Evocative** - Tending or having the power to evoke.

- **Evolution** - A gradual process in which something changes into a different and usually more complex or better form; The process of developing.

- **Excursion** - A usually short journey made for pleasure; an outing; A roundtrip on a passenger vehicle at a special low fare; A group taking a short pleasure trip together; A diversion or deviation from a main topic; a digression.

- **Exegesis** - Critical explanation or analysis, especially of a text; explanation or critical interpretation of a text, esp of the Bible Compare.

- **Exegesis** - critical interpretation of a text

- **Exultation** - the act or condition of rejoicing greatly; the act of exulting or the state of being exultant

- **Facet** - One of numerous aspects, as of a subject.

- **Fascism -** A system of government marked by centralization of authority under a dictator, stringent socioeconomic controls, suppression of the opposition through terror and censorship, and typically a policy of belligerent nationalism and racism; A political philosophy or movement based on or advocating such a system of government; Oppressive, dictatorial control.

- **Fecund** - Capable of producing offspring or vegetation; fruitful; Marked by intellectual productivity.

- **Fiat** - An arbitrary order or decree; Authorization or

sanction

- **Foster** - To bring up; nurture; To promote the growth and development of; cultivate; Providing parental care and nurture to children not related through legal or blood ties.

- **Frenetic** - Wildly excited or active; frantic; frenzied.

- **Galvanizing** - to stimulate or shock with an electric current; to arouse to awareness or action; to coat (iron or steel) with rust-resistant zinc.

- **Gamine** - An often homeless girl who roams about the streets; an urchin; A girl or woman of impish appeal; a slim and boyish girl or young woman; an elfish tomboy

- **Gaucherie** - Tactless or Awkward Action

- **Genre** - a type or class; a category of artistic composition, as in music or literature, marked by a distinctive style, form, or content; a realistic style of painting that depicts scenes from everyday life.

- **Germane** - pertinent

- **Glib** - Performed with a natural, offhand ease; Characterized by fluency of speech or writing that often suggests insincerity, superficiality, or a lack of concern.

- **Hack** - to cope with successfully; manage.

- **Hagiography** - the study of saints

- **Harrow** - any of various implements used to level the ground, stir the soil, break up clods, destroy weeds, etc., in soil; to plunder; sack.

- **Hermeneutics** - the science of interpretation and explanation, especially the branch of theology that deals with the general principles of Biblical interpretation

- **Heuristic** - Discover, Reveal

- **Heuristic** - helping to learn; guiding in discovery or investigation; encouraging a person to learn, discover, or solve problems on his or her own, as by experimenting, evaluating possible answers or solutions, or by trial and error.

- **Hitherto** - Until this time; to this place or point

- **Homilies** - a sermon, especially one intended to edify a congregation on a practical matter and not intended to be a theological discourse; a tedious moralizing lecture or admonition; an inspirational saying or platitude.

- **Hoo-ha** - A fuss; a disturbance; A chortle or laugh; a noisy commotion or fuss.

- **Hortatory** - excitatory/exhortation

- **Hubris** - Overbearing pride or presumption; arrogance; pride or arrogance; excessive pride or self-confidence; arrogance.

- **Huckster** - One who sells wares or provisions in the

street; a peddler or hawker; One who uses aggressive, showy, and sometimes devious methods to promote or sell a product; One who writes advertising copy, especially for radio or television; To promote or attempt to sell (a commercial product, for example) in an overaggressive or showy manner.

- **Humus** - A brown or black organic substance consisting of partially or wholly decayed vegetable or animal matter that provides nutrients for plants and increases the ability of soil to retain water.

- **Hyperbole** - A figure of speech in which exaggeration is used for emphasis or effect; a deliberate exaggeration used for effect.

- **Ideology** - The body of ideas reflecting the social needs and aspirations of an individual, group, class, or culture; A set of doctrines or beliefs that form the basis of a political, economic, or other system.

- **Ignoble** - Not noble in quality, character, or purpose; base or mean; Not of the nobility; common.

- **Imbue** - permeate

- **Immemorial** - Reaching beyond the limits of memory, tradition, or recorded history; originating in the distant past; ancient.

- **Immoderate** - Exceeding normal or appropriate bounds; extreme; lacking in moderation; excessive.

- **Impecunious** - Lacking money; penniless.

- **Impoverished** - Reduced to poverty; poverty-stricken; Deprived of natural richness or strength; limited or depleted.

- **Impoverished** - Reduced to poverty; poverty-stricken; Deprived of natural richness or strength; limited or depleted; (of a country or region) having few trees, flowers, wild animals, etc.

- **Improvidence** - Not providing for the future; thriftless; Rash; incautious.

- **Incendiary** - causing or capable of causing fire; of or containing chemicals that produce intensely hot fire when exploded; tending to inflame; inflammatory

- **Inchoate** - Incomplete, just Started, Partly in existence

- **Indiscernible** - Difficult or impossible to discern or perceive; imperceptible; incapable of being discerned; scarcely discernible or perceptible.

- **Inelegancies** - Lack of refinement or polish; the quality or state of being inelegant; lack of elegance.

- **Infantry** - The branch of an army made up of units trained to fight on foot; Soldiers armed and trained to fight on foot; A unit, such as a regiment, of such soldiers.

- **Insouciance** - lack of care or concern; indifference.

- **Intelligentsia** - intellectuals considered as a group or class, esp. as a cultural, social, or political elite

- **Interface** - A surface forming a common boundary between adjacent regions, bodies, substances, or phases; A point at which independent systems or diverse groups interact.

- **Invidious** - Tending to rouse ill will, animosity, or resentment; Containing or implying a slight; discriminatory; Envious.

- **Juggernaut** - Something, such as a belief or institution, that elicits blind and destructive devotion or to which people are ruthlessly sacrificed; An overwhelming, advancing force that crushes or seems to crush everything in its path; any terrible force, esp one that destroys or that demands complete self-sacrifice.

- **Juxtaposed** - To place side by side, especially for comparison or contrast.

- **Juxtaposition** - The act or an instance of juxtaposing or the state of being juxtaposed; an act or instance of placing close together or side by side, esp. for comparison or contrast; the state of being close together.

- **Languorously** - Lack of physical or mental energy; listlessness; A dreamy, lazy mood or quality; Oppressive quiet or stillness.

- **Largess/ Largesse** - something given to someone without expectation of a return

- **Lather** - A foam formed by soap or detergent agitated in water, as in washing or shaving; Froth formed by profuse sweating, as on a horse; A condition of anxious or heated discomposure; agitation.

- **Legitimacy** - The quality or fact of being legitimate; the state of being legitimate.

- **Liberation** - The act of liberating or the state of being liberated; The act or process of trying to achieve equal rights and status.

- **Lilliputian** - A very small person or being; Very small; diminutive; Trivial; petty.

- **Machiavellian -** of or relating to the alleged political principles of Niccolò Machiavelli (1469-1527), Florentine statesman and political philosopher; cunning, amoral, and opportunist; a cunning, amoral, and opportunist person, esp a politician.

- **Magnate** - A powerful or influential person, especially in business or industry; a person of power and rank in any sphere, esp in industry; a member of the upper chamber in certain European parliaments, as in Hungary.

- **Manichaean View** - theology of struggle of good v. evil

- **Manifest** - Clearly apparent to the sight or understanding; obvious; To show or demonstrate plainly; reveal; To be evidence of; prove.

- **Manifold** - Marked by variety

- **Megalomania** - feelings of personal omnipotence & grandeur

- **Messiah** - the promised and expected deliverer of the Jewish people.

- **Messianic** - of or relating to the Messiah, his awaited deliverance of the Jews, or the new age of peace expected to follow this; of or relating to Jesus Christ or the salvation believed to have been brought by him.

- **Minimus -** a creature or being that is the smallest or least significant.

- **Mitigate** - To moderate (a quality or condition) in force or intensity; alleviate; To become milder.

- **Modernity** - The state or quality of being modern; the quality or state of being modern.

- **Mogul** - a small hard mound or bump on a ski slope; an important or powerful person; (Historical Terms) a member of the Muslim dynasty of Indian emperors established by Baber in 1526.

- **Monolog** - A dramatic soliloquy; A continuous series of jokes or comic stories delivered by one comedian; A long speech made by one person, often monopolizing a conversation.

- **Moribund** - Approaching death; about to die; On the verge of becoming obsolete.

- **Mundane** - of, relating to, or typical of this world; secular; relating to, characteristic of, or concerned with commonplaces; ordinary.

- **Myopic** - A visual defect in which distant objects appear blurred because their images are focused in front of the retina rather than on it; nearsightedness. Also called short sight; Lack of discernment or long-range perspective in thinking or planning.

- **Nabulous** – Hazy, vague, confused.

- **Nadir** - A point on the celestial sphere directly below the observer, diametrically opposite the zenith; The lowest point.

- **Necrosis** - Death of cells or tissues through injury or disease, especially in a localized area of the body.

- **Neurasthenia** - A psychological disorder characterized by chronic fatigue and weakness, loss of memory, and generalized aches and pains, formerly thought to result from exhaustion of the nervous system. No longer in scientific use.

- **Non sequitur** - An inference or conclusion that does not follow from the premises or evidence; A statement that does not follow logically from what preceded it.

- **Nosology** - The branch of medicine that deals with the classification of diseases; A classification of diseases.

- **Nostrums** - A medicine whose effectiveness is

unproved and whose ingredients are usually secret; a quack remedy; A favorite but usually ineffective remedy for problems or evils.

- **Novel(ty)** - A fictional prose narrative of considerable length, typically having a plot that is unfolded by the actions, speech, and thoughts of the characters; Strikingly new, unusual, or different.

- **Nutshell** - The shell enclosing the meat of a nut; *(Idiom)* in a nutshell: In a few words; concisely.

- **Obfuscation** - confusion

- **Odyssey** - The younger of the two surviving ancient Greek epic poems, traditionally ascribed to Homer but containing much orally transmitted material composed over several centuries, and concerning the adventures and ordeals of the Greek warrior Odysseus after the fall of Troy as he struggles to return home and reestablish himself as king of Ithaca; An extended adventurous voyage or trip; An intellectual or spiritual quest; a Greek epic poem, attributed to Homer (c. 800 bc), describing the ten-year homeward wanderings of Odysseus after the fall of Troy; any long eventful journey.

- **Oeuvres** - a work of art; The sum of the lifework of an artist, writer, or composer

- **Oligarchy** - Power in Hand of Few

- **Orchestrating** - To compose or arrange (music) for performance by an orchestra; To arrange or control the elements of, as to achieve a desired overall effect.

- **Ostensible Profundity** – Professed

- **Panegyric** - formal or elaborate praise

- **Pangloss** - a person who views a situation with unwarranted optimism;

- **Panoply** - A splendid or striking array; Ceremonial attire with all accessories; Something that covers and protects; The complete arms and armor of a warrior.

- **Pantheon** - A temple dedicated to all gods; All the gods of a people considered as a group; A public building commemorating and dedicated to the heroes and heroines of a nation; A group of persons most highly regarded for contributions to a field or endeavor.

- **Paradigm** - One that serves as a pattern or model; A set or list of all the inflectional forms of a word or of one of its grammatical categories; A set of assumptions, concepts, values, and practices that constitutes a way of viewing reality for the community that shares them, especially in an intellectual discipline.

- **Pareidolia** - a psychological phenomenon involving a vague and random stimulus (often an image or sound) being perceived as significant, a form of apophenia.

- **Parsimony** - extreme frugality

- **Pathognomonic** - Characteristic or symptomatic of a particular disease or condition.

- **Pathos** - A quality, as of an experience or a work of art, that arouses feelings of pity, sympathy, tenderness, or sorrow; The feeling, as of sympathy or pity, so aroused.

- **Pedagogical (Teaching)** - Of, relating to, or characteristic of pedagogy; Characterized by pedantic formality.

- **Pedagogy** - Art of Teaching

- **Pedantic** - Characterized by a narrow, often ostentatious concern for book learning and formal rules; of, relating to, or characterized by pedantry.

- **Pejorative** - Having tendency to make worse

- **Pell-mell** - In mingled confusion

- **Peradventure** - Perhaps; perchance; Chance or uncertainty; doubt.

- **Periwigs** - A wig, especially a peruke.

- **Perspicacious** - of acute mental vision or discernment keen

- **Perspicacity** - intelligence manifested by being astute (as in business dealings)

- **Pervade** - To be present throughout; permeate; to become spread throughout all parts of.

- **Philistine** - A member of an Aegean people who settled ancient Philistia around the 12th century BC; A smug, ignorant, especially middle-class person who is regarded as being indifferent or antagonistic to artistic and cultural values; One who lacks knowledge in a specific area; a person who is unreceptive to or hostile towards culture, the arts, etc.; a smug boorish person.

- **Philistines** - A member of an Aegean people who settled ancient Philistia around the 12th century B.C; a person who is unreceptive to or hostile towards culture, the arts, etc.; a smug boorish person.

- **Picayune** - Of little value or importance; paltry; Petty; mean; A Spanish-American half-real piece formerly used in parts of the southern United States; A five-cent piece; Something of very little value; a trifle.

- **Pince-nez** - Eyeglasses clipped to the bridge of the nose.

- **Placate** - Smooth ESP. by Concessions

- **Poignantly** - profoundly moving; touching; physically painful; keenly distressing to the mind or feelings; piercing; incisive; neat, skillful, and to the point; astute and pertinent; relevant; agreeably intense or stimulating

- **Polarize** - To induce polarization in; impart polarity to; To cause to concentrate about two conflicting or contrasting positions; To acquire polarity; To cause polarization of light.

- **Polemic** - A controversial argument, especially one refuting or attacking a specific opinion or doctrine; A person engaged in or inclined to controversy, argument, or refutation.

- **Polemic** - Art of debate/disputation

- **Polyglot** - Speaking, writing, written in, or composed of several languages; A person having a speaking, reading, or writing knowledge of several languages; A book, especially a Bible, containing several versions of the same text in different languages; A mixture or confusion of languages.

- **Polymath** - A person of great or varied learning.

- **Polytomy** - A division into many members.

- **Postures** - A position of the body or of body parts; An attitude; a pose; A characteristic way of bearing one's body; carriage; A frame of mind affecting one's thoughts or behavior; an overall attitude.

- **Posturing** - to assume an exaggerated or unnatural pose or mental attitude; attitudinize; to assume a pose; to put into a specific posture; pose.

- **Pragmatic** - Dealing or concerned with facts or actual occurrences; practical; Relating to or being the study of cause and effect in historical or political events with emphasis on the practical lessons to be learned from them.

- **Précis** - Concise summary of essential point

- **Precocious** - Manifesting or characterized by unusually early development or maturity, especially in mental aptitude; Blossoming before the appearance of leaves; ahead in development, such as the mental development of a child.

- **Predicated** - to base or establish (a statement or action, for example); to state or affirm as an attribute or quality of something; to carry the connotation of; imply; logic to make (a term or expression) the predicate of a proposition; to proclaim or assert; declare.

- **Pretence** - the act of pretending; a false display; affectation; a claim, esp a false one, to a right, title, or distinction; make-believe or feigning; a false claim or allegation; pretext.

- **Procrustean** - Producing or designed to produce strict conformity by ruthless or arbitrary means; tending or designed to produce conformity by violent or ruthless methods.

- **Procrustean Bed** - plan or scheme to produce uniformity or conformity by arbitrary or violent methods. Origin: after Procrustes

- **Profane** - Marked by contempt or irreverence for what is sacred; Nonreligious in subject matter, form, or use; secular; Not admitted into a body of secret knowledge or ritual; uninitiated; Vulgar; coarse; To treat with irreverence; To put to an improper, unworthy, or degrading use; abuse.

- **Profligate** – Wildly extravagant, self-indulgent .

- **Promulgation** - To make known (a decree, for

example) by public declaration; announce officially; To put (a law) into effect by formal public announcement.

- **Prophylactic** - Acting to defend against or prevent something, especially disease; protective; A prophylactic agent, device, or measure, such as a vaccine or drug; A contraceptive device, especially a condom.

- **Proselytizing** - To induce someone to convert to one's own religious faith; To induce someone to join one's own political party or to espouse one's doctrine; To convert (a person) from one belief, doctrine, cause, or faith to another.

- **Prostitute** - One who solicits and accepts payment for sex acts; One who sells one's abilities, talent, or name for an unworthy purpose.

- **Protean** - Readily assuming diff. roles or shape

- **Provocate – to provoke**

- **Pygmalion** - A king of Cyprus who carved and then fell in love with a statue of a woman, which Aphrodite brought to life as Galatea.

- **Pyrotechnics** - The art of manufacturing or setting off fireworks. Also called pyrotechny; A fireworks display; A brilliant display, as of rhetoric or wit, or of virtuosity in the performing arts.

- **Quod erat demonstrandum -** Which as to be demonstrated

- **Raptures** - The state of being transported by a lofty emotion; ecstasy; An expression of ecstatic feeling. Often used in the plural; The transporting of a person from one place to another, especially to heaven; To enrapture.

- **Reconstituted** - To provide with a new structure; To bring (a liquid in concentrated or powder form) to normal strength by adding water; to restore (food, etc.) to its former or natural state or a semblance of it, as by the addition of water to a concentrate.

- **Regimes** - A form of government; A prevailing social system or pattern; The period during which a particular administration or system prevails; A regulated system, as of diet and exercise; a regimen.

- **Relentless** - unyielding in severity or strictness; unrelenting; steady and persistent; unremitting.

- **Repugnance** - Extreme dislike or aversion; The relationship of contradictory terms; inconsistency; strong distaste or aversion.

- **Robust** - Full of health and strength; vigorous; Powerfully built; sturdy; Requiring or suited to physical strength or endurance; Rough or crude; boisterous; Marked by richness and fullness; full-bodied.

- **Rubric** - Title, Heading, Category

- **Sacerdotal** - Relating to priests.

- **Sagacious** - of keen and farsighted penetration and judgment, discerning

- **Salutary** - Effecting or designed to effect an improvement; remedial; Favorable to health; wholesome; promoting or intended to promote health.

- **Salvos** - A simultaneous discharge of firearms; The simultaneous release of a rack of bombs from an aircraft; The projectiles or bombs thus released; Something resembling a release or discharge of bombs or firearms.

- **Sanctified** - to set apart for sacred use; consecrate; to make holy; purify; to give religious sanction to, as with an oath or vow; to give social or moral sanction to; to make productive of holiness or spiritual blessing

- **Sarabande** - A fast, erotic dance of the 16th century of Mexico and Spain; A stately court dance of the 17th and 18th centuries, in slow triple time; The music for either of these dances.

- **Scenario** - An outline of the plot of a dramatic or literary work; A treatment for a screenplay; An outline or model of an expected or supposed sequence of events.

- **Schadenfreude** - Pleasure derived from the misfortunes of others; delight in another's misfortune.

- **Sclerosis** - a hardening of a body tissue or part, or an increase of connective tissue or the like at the expense of more active tissue; a hardening of a plant tissue or cell wall by thickening or becoming woody.

- **Screed** - A long monotonous speech or piece of writing; A strip of wood, plaster, or metal placed on a wall or pavement as a guide for the even application of plaster or concrete; A layer or strip of material used to level off a horizontal surface such as a floor; A smooth final surface of a substance, such as concrete, applied to a floor.

- **Scurrilous** - Given to the use of vulgar, coarse, or abusive language; foul-mouthed; Expressed in vulgar, coarse, and abusive language; grossly or obscenely abusive or defamatory; characterized by gross or obscene humor.

- **Sensuous** - Of, relating to, or derived from the senses; Appealing to or gratifying the senses; aesthetically pleasing to the senses.

- **Serendipity** - luck that takes the form of finding valuable or pleasant things that are not looked for.

- **Shellacked** - to coat or treat (an article) with a shellac varnish; A thin varnish made by dissolving this substance in denatured alcohol, used to finish wood.

- **Shibboleth** - a peculiarity of pronunciation, usage, or behavior that distinguishes a particular group; a slogan; catchword; a common saying or belief with little current meaning or truth

- **Sic** - intentionally written; Thus; so. Used to indicate that a quoted passage, especially one containing an error or unconventional spelling, has been retained in its original form or written intentionally.

- **Simulacra** - An image or representation; An unreal or vague semblance; a slight, unreal, or vague semblance of something; superficial likeness; an effigy; image; representation.

- **Simulacrum** - likeness/weak imitation

- **Sine Qua Non** - An essential element or condition; an essential condition or requirement; an indispensable or essential condition, element, or factor.

- **Sloth** - Aversion to work or exertion; laziness; indolence; any slow-moving, arboreal tropical American edentate of the family Bradypodidae, having hooklike claws and usu. hanging upside down.

- **Slynx** - evil monster

- **Solipsistically** - **P**ertaining to the theory that the self is the only thing that can be known and verified; The theory or view that the self is the only reality.

- **Sovereign** - One that exercises supreme, permanent authority, especially in a nation or other governmental unit; A nation that governs territory outside its borders; A gold coin formerly used in Great Britain; Self-governing; independent; Having supreme rank or power; Paramount; supreme.

- **Spurious** - Lacking authenticity or validity in essence or origin; not genuine; false; Of illegitimate birth; Botany

Similar in appearance but unlike in structure or function. Used of plant parts.

- **Sterile** - Not producing or incapable of producing offspring; Free from live bacteria or other microorganisms; Lacking imagination, creativity, or vitality; Lacking the power to function; not productive or effective; fruitless.

- **Stratagem** - A military maneuver designed to deceive or surprise an enemy; A clever, often underhanded scheme for achieving an objective; a plan or trick, esp one to deceive an enemy.

- **Subverted** - To destroy completely; ruin; To undermine the character, morals, or allegiance of; corrupt; To overthrow completely.

- **Suigeneris** - constituting a class alone : unique, peculiar

- **Suttee** - widow throwing self on husband's funeral pyre

- **Sycophancy** - The fawning behavior of a sycophant; servile flattery; the character or conduct of a sycophant.

- **Sycophant** - A servile self-seeker who attempts to win favor by flattering influential people; a self-seeking, servile flatterer; fawning parasite.

- **Symbiosis** - a close, prolonged association between two or more different organisms of different species that may, but does not necessarily, benefit each member; a relationship of mutual benefit or dependence.

- **Syncopating** - to subject (musical rhythm) to syncopation; to shorten by syncope

- **Tangent** - touching; almost irrelevant.

- **Tantamount** - Equivalent in effect or value; as good (as); equivalent in effect (to).

- **Tautological** - Needless repetition of the same sense in different words; redundancy; An instance of such repetition.

- **Tautology** - Define to the point of meaninglessness

- **Tedium** - The quality or condition of being tedious; tediousness or boredom.

- **Tenuous** - long and thin; slender; having a thin consistency; dilute; having little substance; flimsy.

- **Thanatos** - Death as a personification or as a philosophical notion; the death instinct, esp. as expressed in violent aggression.

- **Totem** - A venerated emblem or symbol; A representation of such an object; A social group having a common affiliation to such an object; An animal, plant, or natural object serving among certain tribal or traditional peoples as the emblem of a clan or family and sometimes revered as its founder, ancestor, or guardian.

- **Trajectory** - The path of a projectile or other moving body through space; A chosen or taken course;

Mathematics A curve that cuts all of a given family of curves or surfaces at the same angle.

- **Trammel** - A tool for restraining a horse's ambling; The trammel of Archimedes, a tool for drawing ellipses; A type of fishing net.

- **Trenchant** - Sharply perceptive; Forceful, effective, and vigorous; Caustic; cutting; Distinct; clear-cut.

- **Trepidation** - A state of alarm or dread; apprehension; An involuntary trembling or quivering; a condition of quaking or palpitation, esp. one caused by anxiety.

- **Tumultuous** - Characterized by tumult; noisy and disorderly; Tending to cause tumult; Confusedly or violently agitated.

- **Unsuccored** – Giving no relief or stopping.

- **Verisimilitude** - The quality of appearing to be true or real; Something that has the appearance of being true or real

- **Vindication** - The act of vindicating or condition of being vindicated; The defense, such as evidence or argument, that serves to justify a claim or deed.

- **Visage** - the face or facial expression of a person; countenance; appearance; aspect

- **Vis-à-vis** - Face to face; in company; as compared with

- **Vitiate** - contaminate, Debase, Pervert

- **Vitriol** - Bitterly abusive feeling or expression.

- **Volleys** - A simultaneous discharge of a number of missiles; The missiles thus discharged; A bursting forth of many things together.

- **Vulgarization** - To make vulgar; debase; To disseminate widely; popularize.

- **Whirligig** - Any of various spinning toys; A carousel; a merry-go-round; Something that continuously whirls; The whirligig beetle.

- **Woeful** - Affected by or full of woe; mournful; Causing or involving woe; Deplorably bad or wretched; expressing or characterized by sorrow; bringing or causing woe.

- **Xenophobe** - A person unduly fearful or contemptuous of that which is foreign, especially of strangers or foreign peoples; (Sociology) a person who hates or fears foreigners or strangers.

- **Zenith** - The point on the celestial sphere that is directly above the observer; The upper region of the sky; The highest point above the observer's horizon attained by a celestial body; The point of culmination; the peak.

- **Zentrepreneur** - Business person who channels good vibes.

Appendix C
Your Library Card for a Lifetime

Wouldn't it be great if…

…there was a way to not have to be on a million ListServs getting two million emails, most of which are not helpful…but still be able to stay on top of what's going on and important to you?

…and to not have to worry about missing something important while away on vacation from email or just during busy times?

For the first time, you can benefit from my almost daily review of over two dozen newsfeeds and print publications where I collect the best content I come across that is relevant to the Lifetime Library and to you. Then two to four times a month I upload this content into a special DropBox account that I link to you. You can then read it when it convenient for you. It's searchable too! You can rest assured you will never miss anything of importance to developing your practice again.

The result is that you have access to an ever-updating-obsolete-proof digital library. As a writer you'll have access to great content on

- Publishing

- Presenting

- Social media Tools

- Marketing

- Life Hacks

- And much more…

It doesn't get much easier than that! The screen shot is a sampling of what the current content looks like. As of this writing there are over 300 full text articles with links in the library. This is a screenshot to give you a feel for the sheer volume, but don't worry everything is catalogued and neatly organized.

With your **Library Card for a Lifetime** you will have complete access to the tools, articles, and materials that I have found useful in designing my life and in accomplishing what I have thus far. And you just subscribe

once and read for a lifetime! Where else can you do that? Yup, no annual renewal! No renewal ever!

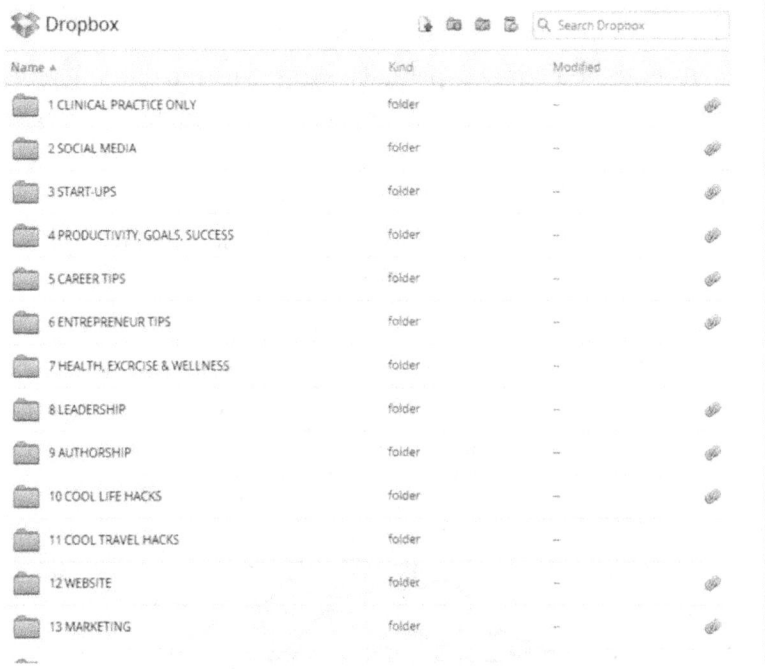

I am committed to doing this for the rest of my life. And if every now and then you'd like to make a donation (a la Wikipedia model), then thanks in advance!

So for $75, you are good to go. Forever. Really. Just go to PayPal https://www.paypal.com and direct your payment to drchrisstout@gmail.com Once I hear from PayPal, I'll send you the DropBox links, and bingo, you are good to go!

ABOUT THE AUTHOR

Dr. Chris Stout is a licensed clinical psychologist and has a diverse background in various domains. He is the Founding Director of the Center for Global Initiatives (CenterForGlobalInitiatives.org) which was ranked as a **Top Healthcare Nonprofit** by GreatNonprofits.org (2011). His entrepreneurial experience is demonstrated in multiple start-ups that include the areas of financial management, healthcare centers, engineering, two dot-coms, real estate, and executive coaching (with a top-tier client list that includes Oracle). He also is a Clinical Full Professor in the College of Medicine, Department of Psychiatry; an Advisory Board Member to the College of Medicine's Center for Global Health; a Fellow in the School of Public Health Leadership Institute, and is a Core Faculty at the International Center on Responses to Catastrophes at the University of Illinois, Chicago. He also holds an academic appointment in Northwestern University Feinberg School of Medicine's Center for Global Health and the Department of Psychiatry and Behavioral Sciences' Mental Health Services and Policy Program, and was a Visiting Professor in the Department of Health Systems Management at Rush University. He served as a Non-Governmental Organization Special Representative to the United Nations. He was appointed by the Secretary of the US Department of Commerce to the Board of Examiners for the Baldrige National Quality Award. He is on the Advisory Board of the American Board of Independent Medical Examiners, and numerous other organizations. He holds the distinction of being one of only 100 world-wide leaders appointed to the World Economic Forum's Global Leaders of Tomorrow 2000 – joining the ranks of Tony Blair, Jody Foster, Bill Gates, R. J. Rowling, and Lance Armstrong, and he was an Invited Faculty at the Annual Meeting in Davos. He was invited by the Club de Madrid and Safe-Democracy to serve on the Madrid-11 Countering Terrorism Task Force. He is the founder of GordianKnot, LLC, an executive leadership consultancy and he currently runs the Department of Research for a national sports and rehabilitation medicine organization with $300M in annual revenues.

Dr. Stout is a Fellow in three Divisions of the American Psychological Association, past-President of the Illinois Psychological Association, and is a Distinguished Practitioner in the National Academies of Practice. He was appointed as a Special (Citizen) Ambassador and Delegation Leader to South Africa and Eastern Europe by the Eisenhower Foundation. He serves as Acquisitions Editor for the *Journal of Disability Medicine*, and is the Series Editor of *Contemporary Psychology* (Praeger) and *"Getting Started"* (Wiley & Sons*).* He produced the critically acclaimed four volume set *The Psychology of Terrorism* and more recently, the highly praised and award–winning three volume set, *The New Humanitarians*, and is an Amazon.com Best Selling Author (reaching a #5 ranking). Additionally, he has published or presented over 300 papers and 30 books/manuals on various topics in psychology, including the popular *Evidence-Based Practice* (Wiley & Sons, 2005, with R. Hayes). His works have been translated into 8 languages. He has lectured across the nation (including being invited to share the dais with Nobel Laureate, Dr. Jody Williams on World Health Day, 2013) and internationally in over 20 countries, and visited 6 continents and over 80 countries. He was noted as being *"one of the most frequently cited psychologists in the scientific literature"* in a study by Hartwick College. He is the 2004 winner of the American Psychological Association's International Humanitarian Award, the 2006 recipient of the Illinois Psychological Association's Humanitarian Award, the 2008 recipient of the Psychologists for Social Responsibility's Humanitarian Award, and the 2009 winner of APA's Division on International Psychology's Outstanding Psychologist Award. He is an inaugural Inductee into his high school's, Purdue University's, and the American Motorcyclist Association's Hall of Fame.

He has served as Chief of Psychology, Director of Research, and Senior VP of an integrated behavioral healthcare system during a 15 year tenure. He served as Illinois' first Chief of Psychological

Services for the Department of Human Services/Division of Mental Health—having made him the highest ranking psychologist in the State of Illinois and a committed reformer of psychology within the governmental setting. He also served as Chief Clinical Information Officer for the State's Division of Mental Health in 2004—a Cabinet-level position. He is the first psychologist to have an invited appointment to the Lake County Board of Health. The breadth of his work ranges from having served as a judge for Dean Kamen's FIRST Robotics competitions, to serving on the Young Leaders Forum of the Chicago Community Trust. His humanitarian activities include going on international missions with the Flying Doctors of America to Vietnam, Rwanda, Peru, and the Amazon; War Child in Russia; having worked with the Kovler Center (for Refugee Survivors of Torture), Amnesty International, RWJ Foundation, the Elizabeth Morse Charitable Trust, and Psychologists for Social Responsibility. He founded a kindergarten for AIDS orphaned children in Tanzania and continues as a consultant. He also was a delegate at the State of the World Forum in Belfast. He is a signatory to the UN's 50th Anniversary of the Universal Declaration of Human Rights. He is the inventor of the *"52 Ways to Change the World"* card deck. He is listed in *Fast Co.'s* Global Fast 50 nominees and in TED Conferences Founder Richard Saul Wurman's *"Who's Really Who, 1000: The Most Creative Individuals in America."* Purdue School of Engineering named a scholarship in his honor for students conducting research, service or international projects. He has won awards for public service announcements he's written and produced as well as for his photography—one was displayed in the Smithsonian.

Dr. Stout was educated at Purdue, The University of Chicago's Graduate School of Business, and Forest Institute, gaining over twenty-four awards and four scholarships; including, the Purdue Distinguished Academic Performance Award, the Purdue Alumni Association Distinguished Service Award, and Valedictorian of his doctoral class. He obtained post-doctoral experience at Harvard Medical School as a Fellow in neuro-developmental behavioral pediatrics. He has received four additional doctorates (*honoris causa*) in clinical psychology, two Doctor of Humane Letters, and from Purdue School of Engineering, a Doctor of Technology. He was awarded "Distinguished Alumni of the Year from Purdue University" in 1991, Federal Advocacy awards from AAP (1997) and APA (1998), APA's Heiser Award (1999), and IPA's Distinguished Psychologist of the Year (1999) in addition to over 30 other post-doctoral awards.

He has been interviewed on many radio, cable, local, and national television programs (e.g., CNBC, CNN, WGN, NBC, PBS, NPR, Medical Rounds, Chicago Tonight, CL-TV, Oprah, Eye On Harvard, Christina, Bertise Berry, et al), and by numerous publications *(Time, Chicago Tribune, The Wall Street Journal, New York Times, USA Today, Women's Day, Modern Healthcare, Associated Press, Child Magazine, Chicago Sun-Times, Windy City Sports, NorthShore Magazine, Monitor on Psychology, ...*). He coined the term *"Emmortality"* and numerous registered service-marks. He was an American Delegate and presenter at the 1st International Conference on Unconventional Computing. A unique and distinct honor was his being named one of ten Volunteer's of the Year by *Pioneer Press* in 1999, for his global efforts, and both the Senate and House similarly recognized his work by proclamation of "Dr. Chris E. Stout Week."

His current interests are in the multidisciplinary aspects of global psychology and healthcare, complex systems, evidence-based practice, and battling mediocrity. He's an avid endurance- and adventure-sportsman as an ultra-marathon runner, certified diver (Blue Hole, Great Barrier Reef, narco- and shark-dives), and an devoted (albeit amateur) alpinist, having thus far summited 3 of the world's 7 Summits as well as Mt. Whitney (tallest in 49 states), Mt. Rainier, Yosemite's Half-Dome, Pikes Peak (with his daughter) and he founded SummitsForOthers.org, much of which is documented in his forthcoming book "**A Life In Full: *The* List of A Lifetime.**" He also shows concours-winning vintage BMW motorcycles and

Porsches as well as builds custom café racers, but his greatest joy comes from being with his best friend and wife, Dr. Karen Beckstrand and their two children, Grayson and Annika.

http://DtChrisStout.com

Contributors' Biographies

Ryan Deiss

Ryan Deiss is a well known Internet marketer that has produced many popular reports and sold advanced courses online. He is an expert in social marketing, continuity programs, blogging, web 2.0, email marketing, and is very knowledgeable in how Internet businesses work. He also actively writes on his popular blog, Driving Traffic.

Brian Feinblum

Brian Feinblum has been promoting best-selling authors, self-published books, motivational speakers, major businesses, leading non-profits, and influential trade associations since 1989. He currently serves as the Chief Marketing Officer and Senior Vice President for MEDIA CONNECT.

He has worked with hundreds of diverse and unique clients across many industries. Brian is instrumental in matching new clients with the right services and servicing their needs. He also develops unique services for the company and is respected as one of the best press kit writers in the business.

Prior to joining MEDIA CONNECT, Brian was the Senior Publicist at Lifetime Books for three years. Notable clients included magician David Copperfield and best-selling author Og Mandino. A sampling of the media appearances he scheduled for his authors included Oprah,

CNN, and USA Today. He also served as the head of publicity for SPI Books for two years. The stable of authors included the best-selling Dr. Ruth. Featured bookings included Larry King Live, Phil Donahue, Geraldo, Joan Rivers, Sally Jesse Raphael and the Associated Press. Recent experts promoted by Media Connect include acting legend Henry Winkler, comedian Jeff Foxworthy, best-selling parenting expert parenting and relationship expert Hal Runkel, baseball announcer Joe Garagiola, CEO of Lower Manhattan Development Corporation John C. Whitehead, gossip columnist Cindy Adams, and Merrill Lynch Global Philanthropy. He often presents at publishing events, including the Cape Cod Writers Conference and the American Society of Journalists & Authors. His ever-popular book marketing and publicity blog can be found at

http://www.bookmarketingbuzzblog.blogspot.com

Brian resides with his wife, their two children, a bulldog (Daisy) in New Rochelle, a suburb of New York City.

Lindsay Buroker

Lindsay is a full-time independent fantasy author who loves travel, yoga, tennis, and vizslas. Her first novel is available for free as an ebook from B&N, iTunes, & Amazon, and other stores.

http://www.lindsayburoker.com
https://www.facebook.com/LindsayBuroker

Kivi Leroux Miller

Kivi Leroux Miller is president of Nonprofit Marketing Guide.com and author of "The Nonprofit Marketing Guide: High-Impact, Low-Cost Ways to Build Support for Your Good Cause" (June 2010) and "Content Marketing for Nonprofits: A Communications Map for Engaging Your Community, Becoming a Favorite Cause, and Raising More Money" (August 2013).

Through training, coaching and consulting, Kivi helps small nonprofits and small communications departments at large nonprofits make a big impression with smart, savvy marketing, communications, and fundraising. She teaches a weekly webinar series and writes a top-ranked blog on nonprofit communications at Nonprofit Marketing Guide.com. Thousands of nonprofits in all 50 U.S. states, across Canada, and in more than 30 countries have participated in Kivi's webinars.

After many years in the San Francisco Bay Area and Washington, DC, she now lives in rural North Carolina with her husband, two young daughters, three cats, a dog, and countless backyard wildlife. She enjoys writing, volunteering, hiking, vegetarian cooking, and teaching her kids how to bake.

Contact Information
Kivi Leroux Miller
President, NonprofitMarketingGuide.com
319 Becks Church Road
Lexington, NC 27292
www.nonprofitmarketingguide.com
kivi@ecoscribe.com
Office: 336-499-5816 Mobile: 336-870-0251

Click Plan

Click Plan is a product of Zepho Inc, founded by Bala Paranj. He completed his MS in Electrical Engineering from Wichita State University. He has self published software development books. Over a period of 10 years he has used manysoftware solutions for self publishers. However, he became frustrated with the existing solutions. He decided to develop a software as a service product to help self publishers succeed. You can signup for a free two week trial at ww.clickplan.net. You can contact him by email at support@zepho.com.

Steve O'Keefe,

Steve O'Keefe is co-founder and chief operating officer of SixEstate Communications, a marketing firm offering original, expert content written by professional journalists. Steve is a serial entrepreneur, writer, professor, and Internet pioneer. He wrote the bestselling book, "Publicity on the Internet," in 1996, and taught Internet PR at Tulane University from 2001-2011. Steve is co-founder of the International Association of Online Communicators. He was president of AuthorViews (2004-2008) and executive director of Patron Saint Productions (2001-2013). Steve has launched online campaigns for over one thousand books and several of the world's largest publishing brands, including Dr. Seuss, ...For Dummies, Ripley's Believe It or Not!, RealAge, and Wiley InterScience.

C.O.O., SixEstate Communications
Copyright © 2013 by SixEstate Communications LLC
Used With Permission

Source: The Content Marketing Blog at SixEstate
URL of article:
http://sixestate.com/buying-your-way-onto-bestseller-lists/
URL for Steve O'Keefe : http://sixestate.com/about/
URL for SixEstate: http://sixestate.com/services/

CreateSpace Resources

The article Help Readers Discover Your Books on Amazon originally appeared on CreateSpace.com. For more helpful articles and blogs for authors, visit www.createspace.com/resources. Reprinted with permission. © 2013 CreateSpace, a DBA of On-Demand Publishing, LLC. All rights reserved.

Bryan Tracy

Brian Tracy is Chairman and CEO of Brian Tracy International, a company specializing in the training and development of individuals and organizations. Brian's goal is to help people achieve their personal and business goals faster and easier than they ever imagined.

Brian Tracy has consulted for more than 1,000 companies and addressed more than 5,000,000 people in 5,000 talks and seminars throughout the US, Canada and 55 other countries worldwide. As a Keynote speaker and seminar leader, he addresses more than 250,000 people each year.

For more information on Brian Tracy programs, go to: www.briantracy.com